IF GOD HAD A JOB

YAAKOV CADRANEL

If God Had a Job

© Copyright Jacques Yaakov Cadranel

All rights reserved. No part of this book may be reproduced or transmitted in any form or by any means, electronic or mechanical, including photocopying, recording, or by any information storage and retrieval system, without the written permission from the author and publisher.

Published by: SPP Growth: www.SPPGrowth.com

To purchase go to: www.If-God.com

Art & front cover – Sara Cadranel, Bezalel Jerusalem

ISBN: 978-965-93214-0-7

***In gratitude to The Rebbe,
Rabbi Menachem Mendel Schneerson***

All insights in this book, have been inspired by his teachings.

Table of Contents

Purpose of this Book 1
Book Structure 4
Acknowledgements 6

Part I - The Basics of Work-Life 9

1. What's the point and purpose of work? 11
2. Achieving a work-life balance 15
3. Which career should I choose? 19
4. Key behaviours to adopt in pursuing goals 23
5. Making an everlasting impact 27
6. Challenges - finding the joy 31
7. Pathway to personal growth 35
8. Dealing with conflicts and confrontations 39
9. Transform daily mundane interactions 43
10. How to achieve your dreams 47
11. Living according to your values 51
12. Survive and thrive in any culture 55

Part II - Remove Limits To Your Potential 59

13. Work to live, rather than live to work 61
14. Delivering the (apparent) impossible 65
15. Feel free to be who you are 69
16. Dealing with loss of enthusiasm 73
17. Delegation: mastering a double edged sword 77
18. What to do once you become an 'expert' 81
19. How to approach using your unique gifts 85
20. Revealing the potential in others 89
21. Fact: You can't do it by yourself. So How? 93
22. Is it better to be a thinker or a feeler? 97
23. Building cultures of integrity 101

Part III - Developing a Better "Me" 103

- 24 Should I tell people about my strengths? 105
- 25 Feeling the pressure? - How to behave 109
- 26 Dealing with failure 113
- 27 Do I notice my own faults? 117
- 28 Correcting my faults 121
- 29 Pause... where is my work and career going? 125
- 30 Being a "mensch" with tough decisions 129
- 31 How can I change the culture? 133
- 32 Building healthy self-esteem 137
- 33 Taking advice from those you trust 141

Part IV - The Leader Within 145

- 34 Building a sense of belonging for all 147
- 35 Making people feel valued with self-worth 151
- 36 How to impart impactful wisdom 155
- 37 Leadership "101" - Listen first, then follow 159
- 38 Get to the top of your ladder, not the ladder 163
- 39 The ultimate act of responsible behaviour 167
- 40 Instilling confidence versus fear...171
- 41 Taking the lead as a junior 175
- 42 How leaders can persevere with the mission 179
- 43 Leadership when progress stalls 183

Part V - Delivering the Strategy and Mission 185

- 44 Ensuring everyone embraces the mission 187
- 45 Relatability… building connected cultures..............................191
- 46 The Power of the Obedient Follower 195
- 47 Establishing objective clarity 199
- 48 Demotivated? Feeling stuck? Nowhere to go? 203
- 49 How to win...207
- 50 Managing success ...what to do after you win 211
- 51 The art of making strategic decisions......................................215
- 52 How to "max out" on your potential impact 219
- 53 Setting the mission and ambitions 223
- 54 Personal achievement versus team purpose 228

Purpose of this Book

For most of us, a huge portion of our lives is spent at work, "making a living". The best hours of the day, over the prime years in life, are typically dedicated to this pursuit.

Everyone's work-life and career spans a huge range of situations, pressures and challenges. This can often lead to opportunities missed, overwhelm and anxiety, and thus potentially result in stress, low self-esteem, as well as meaningless, hollow work-life experiences.

Over the last thirty years, by learning from my own and observing others successes and failures in work-life, I noticed that successes, for individuals, leaders and organizations, were driven by adopting ancient insights from Chassidic teachings, namely inner dimensions of the Torah/Jewish Bible.

Whether these teachings were adopted consciously or intuitively, the consistent brilliance, insightfulness and relevance of these ancient Chassidic teachings was mind-blowing and transformational.

These observations and revelations, gave birth to this book, *"If God Had a Job"*, to present and offer insights to proactively and consciously provide solutions to help address some of our work-life challenges and open up enormous opportunities.

This is not just for the benefit of any individual who might have a job, but also for leaders and organizations to deliver ambitious strategies and build winning cultures and values.

"If God Had a Job", provides <u>step by step</u> insights and suggestions to practically address some of these aspects, to help make this major aspect of life more successful, meaningful, and impactful. Presented as a workbook, it provides

step by step practical insights and suggestions that enable rapid, almost immediate application and results.

A whole range of actual, "real life" work and career aspects are covered, including:

- For the individual: What type of work should I do; how do I achieve a better work-life balance; dealing with conflicts; how to bring purpose and meaning from my career, as well as how to achieve more all-round success.
- For leaders and organizations: How to be effective leaders, deliver and manage success, as well as develop winning actionable strategies, cultures and core values.

Needless to say, God, as the Creator of the universe, does not *per-se* have a "job". However, the Torah represents not just an accounting of creation and the formation of the Jewish people, but also within it, are insights to God's Divine wisdom to all aspects of life, including work.

In essence the Torah is a guidebook to life itself, enabling an individual to achieve their potential success, purpose, and meaning, whilst positively impacting Creation.

By way of background, these inner dimensions of Divine wisdom, have been brought down through the mystical esoteric analysis of the Hebrew text in the Torah, over two millennium ago, known as "Kabbalah". These ancient insights have, over the last three hundred years or so, been more tangibly explained, into what is broadly known as Chassidus, or Chassidic insights.

Importantly, *"If God Had a Job"* only extracts and distils a minute sample of these Divine wisdoms and applies them to a variety of everyday work-life situations and challenges.

Finally, and fundamental to the forming of this book, each insight is directly inspired from talks and writings of **Rabbi Menachem Mendel Schneerson (1902 -1994)**, of blessed memory, simply known as **"the Rebbe"**, who led the Chassidic movement of Chabad Lubavitch from 1950.

The Rebbe, as well as being a preeminent post holocaust Jewish leader, was a master in teaching Chassidus; tangibly explaining countless practical life lessons of Divine infinite wisdom, for everyday life situations.

The hallmark of the Rebbe's teachings encapsulate infinite Divine wisdom and transform it into practical advice within our finite lives. It is the hope that individuals, leaders and organizations across the globe can benefit from the aspects contained within *"If God Had a Job"*, in leading and developing meaningful successful careers, as well as achieving ambitious value and impact, in a constructive and positive way.

Book Structure

In parallel with each of the fifty four portions of the Torah, fifty four work situation-challenges are considered, providing tangible and easy-to-adopt insights and tools to enable a more impactful, meaningful career.

The fifty four chapters, are apportioned into five sections, corresponding to the "five books of Moses" which form the whole Torah.

The first three sections primarily centre on situations of an individual nature, faced by all employees. The fourth, highlights aspects faced by leaders and teams. The final section addresses the more macro strategic situations and cultural challenges dealt by the CEO and Board, relating to the overall direction of the organization as a whole.

Whilst there are countless lessons and insights within each Torah portion, just one has been selected per chapter. Importantly, this is not an academic text, but rather a practical "workbook", which offers the opportunity for each reader to personalise and adopt the shared insights.

Each chapter has the same structure, namely:

- Title, and brief explanation of the **work situation being addressed**
- **Torah source** (on the facing page) – together with a Chassidic insight, based on a teaching from the Rebbe, providing a solution to the problem being addressed.
- **Suggested approach** and mindset to deal with the challenge, based upon the Rebbe's insight.
- **Potential benefits** and results from the insight.
- **Impact takeaway** - a concluding "one line sound-bite" from the insight.
- **Making it personal** - questions for personal reflection to internalize the insight

- **Role model shout out** - to reflect who in your life has demonstrated the insights, traits and suggested behaviours, and even perhaps trigger you to thank and acknowledge them.

For each chapter, the suggested approach is to first read the work situation being addressed, followed by the Torah source and Chassidic insight on the facing page. Only then, continue reading the chapter's suggested approach and remaining sections.

"Making it personal", and "Role model shout out", are opportunities for you to embed and own the insights for yourself.

"Role model shout out", in particular, enables you to have in mind your personal role models to the suggested behaviours that you might like to adopt. Whether it is someone you know personally, or someone who you have read about, doesn't matter. The key is to try and have someone in mind who inspires you in relation to the insight being covered.

These final two aspects in each chapter are there to enable you, the reader, to internalize and embrace the insights as well as become the "author" of your own personal guidebook. They will hopefully build upon your direct experiences and situations and incorporate the insights that *"If God Had a Job"* might have brought to you.

I hope that the book's structure will help you embrace and embed the Rebbe's teachings, and thus take more positive actions going forward, bringing more meaning, impact and purpose to applying the gift of life within your day to day work-life.

Acknowledgements

First and foremost I thank **the Rebbe**, Rabbi Menachem Mendel Schneerson.

At a time when the world is undergoing ever increasing challenges and confusion, on how a meaningful and impactful life can be embraced, the Rebbe's selfless leadership and teachings have totally transformed my life and that of my family.

These challenges and pressures faced by today's world, have made the key elements of life - family, community and work-life - far more challenging today than ever before.

This book focuses on just one of these, namely that of work-life. It is my deepest wish that your careers, (as well as success of your organizations), will also be transformed and you will reap the benefits as I have from the Rebbe's teachings and explanations of Torah. It's no exaggeration to express that without these teachings, my life would have run another less meaningful or successful course.

Thank you also to my guides and mentors, In addition to our children, they include:

- Rabbi Yossi and Maryashie Deren, who first introduced us to the teachings of the Rebbe, some twenty eight years ago at Chabad of Greenwich, CT. Thank you for your continued love and friendship to this day.
- Rabbi Menachem Junik, "my brother" and our family Rabbi, for the last 25 years. Your spiritual and practical support has been a bedrock within our lives.
- Rabbi Shmuel Lew, for your deep, simple, profound guidance and wisdom, especially during our early years in building our family.

Acknowledgements

Special thank you to my pillars of strength regarding this book:

- **Martin Bandel** – my dear, wise friend of over 25 years. You have always been there for me, and this book is no exception. Thank you for your input and clear logical thinking and critical comprehensive review of key messaging throughout.
- **Rebbetzen Goldie Junik** – a selfless role model, always there for us together with you wonderful husband, our family Rabbi. Regarding this book, I am so very indebted and grateful for your painstaking detailed review of every word, which has so transformed this offering to the readers.
- **Rabbi Alon Moshe Rom** – your depth of knowledge, embodiment and gifted communication of Chassidus and the Rebbe's teachings have so impressed and impacted our family. Thank you for reviewing all Torah aspects and their application to the workplace. Your review has been fundamental to making this book a reality.

Finally, to my **wife and soul mate Atalia**. You are the biggest blessing in my life.

- Thank you for encouraging me throughout my career, as I tried to focus on making value based decisions on principles and humanity, rather than just "earning a living". Cheering me on, as I placed our family first whilst maintaining a work-life balance. Giving me the support not to get sucked into greed, ego and office politics. Reminding me not just be "good at my job", but also approach it as God would wish.
- Thank you for entrusting my decision, at 53 and at the peak of my career, that enough time has been spent on work. You stood by me as I decided that, despite loving every moment of my career, now was the time to say we have "enough", and as the Rebbe said, "now it's time to give back".

Darling Atalia, here's to, God willing, many more years of life together, as we build upon our time since we first met as children, and our 34 years of marriage. Blessed with our five wonderful unique children, their incredible spouses, and now, thank God, the next wave of a new generation.

Yaakov Cadranel – 7th October 2024

Part I
The Basics of Work-Life

Insight from Torah Portion 1 – "Bereshit"

Situation:
All of creation came into being through God's speech, by God saying "Let there be…" … except for the creation of humans.

Quote from the Torah:
Genesis 2:7 - "And the Lord, God formed human out of dust from the ground, and He breathed into his nostrils the soul of life,…". Genesis 3:19 - "… for dust you are, and to dust you will return…"

Chassidic Insight:
Why were humans not created through God's speech like the rest of creation, but rather from dust, the lowest most mundane part of creation? How should one feel about being made from simple dust?

All of creation keeps within the confines of its created nature, with the exception of humans, as humans can use their unique attributes of wisdom and power of free choice, to "partner" with God in creation.

Having come from dust, the lowest aspect of creation, <u>humans are able to elevate all of creation, even from this lowest point</u>. This task and responsibility, however, poses a challenge, namely, how we deal with the fact that we are made from simple lowly dust.

On the one hand, we can use our free choice to reject or rebel against this lowly origin and dedicate our time on earth to show the world that we are "worth far more than just lowly dust". This can result in focusing our life on amassing riches and wealth of far greater value than dust. This "self-absorbed" material accumulation, however, is meaningless. It does nothing to elevate the world, as all inevitably "returns to dust".

The alternative and correct approach is to <u>humbly embrace</u>, that, despite coming from simple dust, we have the loftiest of all potentials. Namely to utilize the unique human gifts whilst alive, and follow the Creator's wishes, becoming His partner in creation, to positively impact and elevate it.

By focusing on elevating creation, rather than accumulating wealth, our impact will remain eternal, even after we return to dust.

Chapter 1

What's the point and purpose of work?

Situation to address

In life all we have is time. For many, a large part of life is spent at work.

Given this, have you ever considered what the key focus of *your* career should be?

If the primary focus is to make as much money as possible, does that mean that your life should be primarily focused on making money?

It seems that, for many, work is more than just financial survival. And if it is solely about making money to survive, is that all it can offer?

So what is the point of work?

What is its true purpose and potential impact?

Suggested mindset and approach

Be mindful that a career is not just about making money or amassing wealth, but rather one of the most potent ways in which you can engage and make a positive and lasting impact on the world – thereby elevating the world to a better place.

Consider having a primary focus to positively impact work interactions and surroundings rather than just focusing on financial wealth.

Think about what you would like to be remembered for, and the huge range of situations where meaningful, positive, impact can be made in the workplace, in addition to collecting a pay check.

Contemplate which aspects of your career will have a sustainable positive impact even when you've left or "returned to dust".

Develop your career as an opportunity to bring greater good by deploying your unique qualities and attributes.

From these sparks of insight and contemplation, delve deeper into really understanding how you can change and "elevate" your corner of the world by going about your "everyday work".

Consider how this can be put into practise, in the huge array of situations and opportunities that exist within the workplace.

Who can you help? How can your behaviours and interactions create an environment of positivity? Perhaps consider, how you could invest a small portion of your pay check to enable greater positive impact?

Through this deeper understanding of the potential impact that you can make, consider what will it take for you to "act" on this and adapt your behaviours and choices?

Once the approach of applying yourself, and adopting an intent to utilize your work-life to elevate more meaningfulness, becomes a 'habit', it is easier to continue, with regular reflections, on what has been achieved, and what more you can do to create an even greater impact.

Results and benefits

By adopting a primary focus on elevating your work environment, rather than simply focusing on financial gain, you create, and realize, a positive ongoing impact, in addition to earning and amassing financial wealth.

The resulting financial return is oftentimes even greater from adopting a broader, more constructive, approach to work.

This mindset develops the foundation of a meaningful and rewarding work-life and career, as will be further discussed and elaborated upon in this book.

The range of benefits is broad and can include:
- Dropping meaningless pursuits of just accumulating wealth, and thus reducing wasting the precious gift of time and life itself
- Being able to focus on what is really important in your life, resulting in fewer regrets

- Wiser decision-making on what to do, how to behave and where to focus your life, resulting in more positive connections and associations
- More positive, content and happier disposition
- Greater sense of purpose and self-esteem
- Have something "still there" and elevated even when you're gone

Impact takeaway

Work-life offers the potential of taking worthless dust and elevating it, leaving a permanent positive impact upon the world

Making it personal:

1. How do I view my work-life? Is it just about making money and accumulating material possessions?
2. Are my behaviours compromised by being overly focused on my material, perceived, success? Am I proud of the way I behave? How would others describe my behaviours?
3. Do I have awareness of the short-term, immediate, gratification of the material aspects of work "success"?
4. How can I use my career opportunities to realize something with more meaning and sustainable impacts?
5. What am I going to do about it? Am I afraid that adopting such an approach will compromise material success? If so, why? Do I understand how trying to elevate my career environment will also lead to greater personal success, in every way?
6. How and where shall I start taking the first additional step… and how can I continue down this path?
7. Do I wish to gain more insights in building a more meaningful, (successful and rewarding) career by reading the rest of this book?

My role model "shout outs" who…

➢ "Elevated and brought positive, meaningful impact to the world through work-life."

Insight from Torah Portion 2 – "Noah"

Situation:
Noah built an ark, as commanded by God, to protect him and his family from an ensuing flood. The flood waters now approach:

Quotes from the Torah:
- Genesis 7:1 - And the Lord said to Noah, "Come into the <u>ark</u>..."
- Genesis 7:11 - All the springs of the <u>great deep</u> were split, and the windows of the <u>heavens</u> opened up
- Genesis 7:18 - And the waters became powerful…. and the ark moved **<u>upon</u>** *(the surface of)* the waters.

Chassidic Insight:
Why does the Torah state that the ark was "upon" the water? Where else would it be?

To explain:
- The Hebrew word for "ark", is Teiva. Teiva also has a second meaning, namely, "word".
- Powerful waters from the depths of the earth relate to material challenges in life, and those from the heavens non-material, spiritual, ones.

Both of these "powerful waters", or pressures, in our everyday lives can either suck us under, or throw us into the air.

Somehow, Noah, while in his ark, was able to survive and remain <u>upon</u> the surface of the waters, he was able to find a balance between these two forces.

Essentially, we are being taught, that by "<u>coming into the word (Teiva)</u>" of prayer, intent and wisdom, we are able to <u>find balance in our lives</u> between material and spiritual… namely a work-life balance.

Chapter 2

Achieving a work-life balance

Situation to address

Is achieving a work-life balance important to you?... How can you balance the amount of time you spend doing your job versus the amount of time you spend with loved ones or pursuing personal interests and hobbies?

Most people intuitively know that such a balance is key to leading a satisfying and meaningful life. The challenge is <u>how</u> to achieve it.

On the one hand, "all work" leads to burn out, emptiness and dissatisfaction through its "one dimensional" existence. Developing and building families, relationships and other meaningful pursuits pay the price.

On the other hand, solely pursuing meaningful, non-financial, pursuits, without the means and funds to do so, will result in these pursuits not being sustainable.

So, whilst having a work-life balance is a goal and aim by many, it's easier said than done and rarely, if ever, truly achievable in a sustainable manner.

So <u>how</u> can this balance be achieved?

Suggested mindset and approach

If a work-life balance is important or desirable to you, just articulate with <u>words</u> what this means and what it looks like. Embrace these words and "internalise" them to understand what it means in practise, and then act upon it.

In many ways it's that simple.

Most people say they desire a work-life balance but rarely think about how this goal can be realized. Life changing events, (births, marriages, bereavements), or vacations, might offer moments of reflection, but rarely result in tangible, sustainable permanent actions and behaviours.

The goal is to have a **sustainable** balance between work and "meaningful to you" activities outside work.

Many people become engulfed in work, totally consumed by it… whereas some others opt to totally escape from pursuing the material necessities, focusing solely on purely personal desires, be it "spiritual", "meaningful" or just fun pursuits.

Both extremes can result in an unhealthy life balance, either totally *focused* on "earning a living or making money", and the other potentially damaging, by totally *avoiding* the "material responsibilities" and necessities in life.

Developing a mindful and conscious desire to have a balance is a fundamental first step. Articulate to yourself what this means and looks like to you and how you can achieve it. Write down the actions required and verbalise what that balance looks like to you… then act upon it.

Ask yourself, how many hours would this mean at your place of work…, and how many times a week, and when would you want to be doing something more meaningful?

It is important to be specific. Know how you want to spend your time and specifically, what you want to do or achieve in your time, like when to "earn money", and when not.

Refer to and refine this "note to self" on a regular basis. Reflect how you are doing on a weekly basis for about 15-30 minutes. Grade yourself as to how the week has gone… and then review your progress every month. It is important to do this annually as well.,

Results and benefits

Over time, you will see a gradual progress in how "savvy" you have become in allocating your time and how effectively you utilise your most precious resource in life, namely your time.

You will develop an inner wisdom and understanding that it is the quality of work, not the quantity that usually delivers sustainable success. This will, in turn, free you to take time out of work with confidence and without guilt, to pursue other activities important to you.

On the occasion when you might need to put in an "all-nighter", you'll be up for it and not resent it. You will also know when to call it "a day" at work and leave early.

Further benefits of your new clarity and energy will invigorate your work, with more noticeable positivity than before, and even greater impact, than having a one-dimensional primary work focus. Importantly, you will feel less engulfed and consumed by work.

Critically, you will be able to allocate your time, energy and resources to aspects of life outside work on a more regular basis, thus enabling you to feel more satisfied with life itself.

The fact is, the benefits of a work-life balance are huge, and a game changer to your quality of life.

Impact takeaway

A work-life balance requires more effort. But worth it!

It is achieved by considering, reflecting and _entering_ into your own words, articulating what this means and looks like to you, and then acting upon it.

Making it personal - consider:

1. Where am I now regarding a work-life balance?
2. Can I think of any "role models" who have it right, or patently wrong?
3. What does a work-life balance look like for me? Can I articulate it?
4. How can I develop a regular, or even a continual assessment, on work-life balance and phase this into my day, so that it becomes a sustainable aspect of my life?
5. What change can I make tomorrow?

My role model "shout outs" who…

➢ "Achieved a work-life balance."

Insight from Torah Portion 3 – "Lech Lecha"

Situation:

God speaks to Abraham (the first Jew and forefather of the Jewish nation) for the very first time, instructing him on his purpose and mission in life.

Even though at this stage Abraham has already achieved fame and fortune, God's first words to him are:

Quote from the Torah:

Genesis 12:1 - "<u>Go to yourself</u>… to the land that I will <u>show</u> you."

Chassidic Insight:

Why was this strange phrase, "<u>Go to yourself</u>..", chosen as the first words and instruction by God to Abraham? .. and what is the connection to being "<u>shown</u>" something?

God wanted to tell Abraham that despite his "successes" to date, he was about to start a whole new journey in life, which was going to result in realizing an impact far greater than he could ever imagine.

The first step in doing this required Abraham to "<u>go to himself</u>", and start a process of introspection and of understanding his true and unique essence.

His path was going to take him beyond his imagination, hence a place that could only be <u>shown</u> by God.

This would lead to a life which would not only be far more meaningful, but also have an eternal positive impact.

This process of first "going to "yourself" in order to understand your unique strengths and gifts, is a lesson to help reach your full potential and purpose in life.

It requires, first and foremost, understanding the essence of who you are and then following this insight on a path that is true to "who you are".

Chapter 3

Which career should I choose?

Situation to address

Out of the thousands of work / career options which one is right for you?

Where can you make the most impact?

Given the amount of your life spent working, finding the right direction is critical, but how can it be identified?

Suggested mindset and approach

Whilst it may feel overwhelming, given all the choices, the answer and direction is right there within you.

The approach to deciding career direction, <u>first</u> requires the time to just honestly reflect and understand who you really are.

Once this is understood, you should follow a path that is true to your essence.

Importantly, this process is not usually something that you can just "figure out" in a one-off contemplation effort. Rather it requires frequent periodic reflection and self-assessment.

At the heart of this reflection is considering questions such as:
- What do I enjoy doing?
- What am I good at?
- What are my passions?... what do I care about?
- What do others who know me see as my strengths?
- What type of jobs can incorporate at least some of these aspects?
- Where do I see myself in five to ten years?

Essentially, it's less about the job per se, and more about understanding your personal essence. This alone, should give some clear direction as to the most appropriate types of career for you – because they align with your personal strengths.

Results and benefits

In short, developing an insight regarding what "feels" like an enjoyable career, and following the true path for you, will empower you to reach and achieve goals in your life that are beyond your present expectations.

Pursuing a career that centres on your personal "sweet spot" and gifts in life, will inevitably result in a feeling of greater self-worth, joy and satisfaction, with lower levels of stress, compared with "the wrong job" that doesn't speak to you.

Furthermore, the financial gains realized by choosing a path aligned with the true you, can often yield the greatest financial success… and with less stress and effort.

Finally, and critically, one comes to the realisation that a career is not so much about what you do (although it needs to be aligned with your strengths and what you ideally enjoy and are "good at"), but rather how you "feel" about it.

This will lead to satisfaction, positive impact, meaning and purpose.

Critically, by pursuing a path that speaks and resonates with your essence, and continuously assessing and fine tuning your career path so that it speaks to the "true you", you will be able to achieve unimaginable and deeply satisfying achievements, impact and elevated self-worth.

Impact takeaway

Finding the right career path, means "going to yourself" … get it right and you will be able to reach for your stars.

Making it personal:

1. Consider the above suggestions and questions to self, namely:
    a. What do I enjoy doing?

b. What am I good at?
   c. What are my passions?
   d. How can I apply all these aspects within a job?
   e. What do those who know me best think I would excel at?
   f. Where do I see myself (career wise) in 5 to 10 years?
2. Rate how my current job and career path is aligned with my answers
3. Are there any other jobs or career paths that would significantly bring me closer to these answers?
4. What steps and plans could I take to better understand and enable this transition to "my" preferred career, and which will enhance aspects of my life?

My role model "shout outs" who…

➢ "Built a career around their innate strengths and gifts."

Insight from Torah Portion 4 – "Vayeira"

Situation:

Abraham is in the process of fulfilling his life's mission. Three examples of how he behaved in approaching his mission and purpose are described:

Example 1: Hospitality and kindness to strangers - one of the key hallmarks of Abraham's purpose in life. On one particularly hot day he offers three travellers some water and a morsel of bread. This is how he performed his task:

Quote 1: Genesis 18:6-8 - "And Abraham hastened - And he took cream and milk and the calf that he had prepared, and he placed [them] before them, and he was standing over them under the tree, and they ate."

Chassidic Insight 1: Say a little, and do a lot. Whilst offering just a morsel of bread and some water, he prepared a lavish meal.

Example 2: Abraham was walking up a mountain deeply contemplating, his greatest test of all from God, namely the sacrifice of his only son Isaac. Whilst being totally consumed in preparing himself for this task, his son Isaac calls out to him:

Quote 2: Genesis 22:7 - "And he (Abraham) said, "Here I am, my son""

Chassidic Insight 2: No matter what is happening in your life always be aware and attentive to others in need.

Example 3: Abraham, who epitomised loving kindness, was about to carry out his final test from God, namely, to go totally against his nature and sacrifice his beloved son Isaac. Just as he was about to slaughter him an angel cries out to him…

*Quote 3: Genesis 22:12 - "Do not stretch forth your hand to the lad, …. for **now** I know that you are a God fearing man…"*

Chassidic Insight 3: Abraham demonstrated that he was able to go beyond his nature of love and kindness and was able to show severity and discipline if that was what was required of him.

Chapter 4
Key behaviours to adopt in pursuing goals

Situation to address

What are the critical behaviours to adopt when fulfilling your personal goals and missions?

Which behaviours optimize performance to deliver the greatest impact?

Suggested mindset and approach

There are three suggested behaviours and approaches which can help you see and also deliver your "best" performance, or at least "far better", than would otherwise be the case:

1. <u>Say a little, yet do a lot</u>: This might seem obvious, but talking about what you are going to do can take away from the focus and genuine intent to perform whatever it is you need to do. Rather, have an unspoken mindset to deliver "leaps and bounds" more than you said you would do.
2. <u>Always be there for others:</u> Regardless of how busy you might be. Should a colleague genuinely ask you for some help or advice, pause in whatever you are doing and respond. At the very least if it is impossible to help at that moment, explain why you can't give your full attention to them, and when you hope to do so.
3. <u>Don't be limited by your nature:</u> Tendencies, preferences and character traits can be limiting factors to your achievements. When you are in a position of sole responsibility to get something done which falls outside your norm, learn to go beyond your nature as needed.

What these three aspects all have in common is an approach to "dig deep".

In summary, delivering your best comes from digging deep in:
- quiet focus on the task in hand
- engage and always be there for others who need you
- and deepest of all, going beyond your nature to ensure you get done whatever is needed, even if it is outside of your natural skills or personality traits.

Results and benefits

By taking actions and "digging deep", you are <u>habituating yourself to go beyond</u> your comfort zone in performance, which in time <u>becomes your "new norm"</u>, thereby setting a new level of performance and impact.

Most importantly, these three approaches all <u>reduce ego, increase humility, and tap into innate resources</u> and capabilities which can all too easily remain hidden.

Considering each approach:

1. <u>Say a little, do a lot</u> - this mindset invariably results in over delivery of tasks because you are always looking for ways to exceed expectations, and stretch yourself to go "beyond", rather than wasting energy in talking about or "positioning" what you are doing.
2. <u>Always be there for others,</u> shows strength of character. The moments when you are called on for help or advice remind you that *your* work is not all that matters, but rather also being there for other people's needs is critical. This mindset has an uncanny consequence of also stepping out from one's own self-importance, and thereby approaching responsibilities with more humility and impact.
3. <u>Don't be limited by your nature,</u> is probably the most transformational of all. How many truly brilliant leaders are naturally shy or introverted, and yet need to step up to the plate and speak to thousands of people. Regardless, when responsibility calls and there is no one else who can do what's needed, even though it may be contrary to your nature, this is a defining moment to attain a new level in achieving "best performance".

Impact takeaway

Best performance comes from "digging deep" to go over and above. Do more, be there for others and stretch beyond natural limitations.

Making it personal - consider:

1. Can I identify any occasions where I feel I could have done better?
2. What could I have improved?
3. What would it take to operate outside of my comfort zones, and break-through my glass ceilings?
4. How do I rate myself in:
    a. Saying a little, and doing a lot
    b. Always being there for others
    c. Going beyond my nature when necessary
5. What specific actions can I take *right now* to shift my performance under these three headings?

My role model "shout outs" who…

➢ "Went beyond what is required of them."

Insight from Torah Portion 5 – "Chaya Sara"

<u>Situation</u>: Abraham's wife Sara has just passed away. This portion focuses on three things that Abraham did after her passing:
- *Buying the first piece of land in Israel at a highly inflated price as a burial plot for Sara*
- *Finding a wife for their only son Isaac*
- *Making their son Isaac the sole heir, inheritor and successor.*

<u>Quotes from the Torah</u>:
- *Genesis 23:9 "Give me the Machpelah Cave, … for a full price"*
- *Genesis 24:4 "..go to my land and to my birthplace, and you shall take a wife for my son, for Isaac"*
- *Genesis 25:5 "And Abraham gave all that he possessed to Isaac"*

<u>Chassidic Insight</u>:

Why did these three events only take place immediately after the passing of Abraham's wife Sara?

Sara <u>dedicated</u> and lived her life for the land of Israel and her only child Isaac.

The land of Israel and her only child represented her core values, primary purpose and focus in life.

Abraham was so touched and impacted by how his wife Sara earnestly expressed these aspects whilst she was alive, that he felt inspired to continue realising her dreams after her passing.

This resulted in buying the first piece of land in Israel, finding a wife for their son Isaac, and appointing him as his successor.

This teaches us that the way we approach <u>our own</u> values during our life, can have an ongoing impact on successive generations.

Chapter 5

Making an everlasting impact

Situation to address

Most of the time we associate making an impact with being present in a situation.

How can you have a positive impact even whilst not being present?

Moreover, how can you make an *everlasting* positive impact?

Suggested mindset and approach

The answer lies in not just what you do but in how you do it…. Essentially, by earnestly and continuously "living" your values and purpose whilst performing your job.

Everyone has a unique combination of positive traits, core purposes, values and principles. Identify yours and then, genuinely, consciously and naturally bring them into your workplace.

"Living" by your positive values and causes can transform the ongoing impact of your work even after the task is done and even after you have left the organization.

Whatever combination of environmental, human wellbeing, family or nature; identify your key life values and principles. Then, authentically live and express them in how you deliver your "task"/chosen profession.

Results and benefits

Having this approach, as well as still getting the job done, tends to result in additional positive and lasting impacts reflecting *your* important positive values.

Furthermore, your engagement and lasting connection, built with the people around you is enhanced.

Bringing your top "values and passions" to work will make your work more meaningful.

More importantly, it brings a richer, more inspiring "human" dynamic to the workplace, which can sometimes get "all too serious and one dimensional" by being focussed on just getting the job done, with narrow bottom-line results and profits.

This should encourage others to introduce their own "values and passions", thereby transforming the workplace culture to a more engaging and meaningful place to work.

Consequently, staff retention, belonging and engagement can also be significantly enhanced.

Impact takeaway

Bring your special "human" values, qualities and attributes to work. They will last far longer than you or the work being done.

Making it personal - consider:

1. What are my core values or character traits that are most important to me?
2. Do I "live" these values in the workplace, or do I hide them?
3. How could I "live" and share these values in a natural authentic way?

My role model "shout outs" who…

➢ "Made/had an ever lasting impact."

Insight from Torah Portion 6 – "Toldot"

Situation:

Isaac, which in Hebrew means laughter, had a cheerful disposition.

Despite numerous hardships he became very successful. Eventually even his enemy, Abimelech, could see that good fortune was with Isaac.

Quotes from the Torah:

- *Genesis 26:12-13 "And Isaac sowed in that land, and he found in that year a hundred fold, and the Lord blessed him..... the man became great, and he grew constantly greater until he had grown very great"*
- *Genesis 26:26-28 "And Abimelech went to him (Isaac) ...said (to Isaac), "We have seen that the Lord was with you"*

Chassidic Insight:

Isaac had many tough challenges in his life, so why was he named "laughter"?

Firstly, he had a cheerful and positive disposition, which came from trusting that "all is for the best".

Consequently, despite his challenges he was not distracted from worry or concern, allowing all his efforts and energy to be focused on dealing with the issue at hand.

This, in turn, led to an inner positivity and success.

Isaac teaches us that, ultimately, the laughter of life comes - paradoxically - from effort and energy dedicated in dealing positively with our challenges.

Happiness becomes laughter when one is confronted with unpredictable challenges and which, with a positive outlook, can be successfully overcome.

Chapter 6

Challenges – finding the joy

Situation to address

Life is full of challenges.

How can they be approached in order to optimise the outcome?

Suggested mindset and approach

Know deep down and create a mindset that "everything is for the best".

Regardless of how tough or "unfair" a situation might be, keep the environment positive and even joyful amongst your team and colleagues.

Focus hard on the issue at hand with inner determination and positivity.

Push aside any worry or "why me" feelings, as these emotions are just expressions from your ego. Instead, bring out the joy in the challenge.

Results and benefits

Essentially, keeping a positive, cheerful and accepting disposition is critical to sustainable success.

By avoiding worry or self-centred frustration, you avoid the negativity and wasted energy which these emotions carry. (They never bring anything positive.)

Your team and colleagues will be significantly inspired and positively influenced by an unwavering positive mindset which will prevail and, which will "get the job done".

In turn, "team positivity" when facing challenges, will result in more positive outcomes. From this, untold successes can result.

There's nothing more powerful to resolving and dealing with a challenging situation than humbly and positively accepting it for what it is.

Furthermore, a positive attitude enables you to manage the issue rather than have the issue manage you!

Finally, having such a disposition creates an environment and culture that people will want to be a part of and feel engaged and committed to.

Remember, people leave negative leaders and poor cultures, *not* challenges!

Impact takeaway

Think good and it will more often than not be good.

Making it personal - consider:

1. What was my mindset last time I/the team was under pressure or under challenge?
2. Could I have been calmer and more positive?... if so how?
3. Was I hard on the *"issue"* with calmness, confidence and clarity… or was I hard on the *people*, and emotional?
4. Going forward what two to three approaches will I take to be more positive, calm and "light" at work?

My role model "shout outs" who…

> "Constantly had a positive mindset."

Insight from Torah Portion 7 – "Vayeitze"

Situation:

Jacob (Isaac's son and heir) arrives penniless in a foreign land and undergoes 20 years of hardship and challenge whilst working for his corrupt father-in-law, Lavan. Jacob describes some of these challenges to Lavan, just before leaving and returning home to Israel.

Quote from the Torah:

Genesis 31:39-41 ".. I would suffer its loss; from my hand you would demand it, what was stolen by day and what was stolen at night…. I was [in the field] by day when the heat consumed me, and the frost at night, and my sleep wandered from my eyes…. This is twenty years that I have spent in your house. I served you …and you (unfairly) changed my wages ten times.

Chassidic Insight:

Why is so much detail given regarding the hardships experienced by Jacob? Normally the Torah practices a minimalistic approach, unless there is a meaningful lesson behind the details.

These challenges and struggles were Jacob's making. They even merited his name being changed to 'Israel', after which all his descendants as a whole nation was to be named. (Genesis 32:29 – "Your name shall no longer be Jacob but Israel, because you have struggled with God and with man, and you have prevailed).

Despite his challenges Jacob successfully raises a family of 12 upright God fearing children, amasses great wealth and becomes the ultimate founding father of the Jewish people. (Whilst Abraham and Isaac each only had one righteous child, Jacob brought up all 12 sons and one daughter to be righteous).

In summary, it is the challenges in life that reveal and bring to the surface the depths of one's resources, strengths and potential, which transforms the person to a whole higher level of impact. From this detail the Torah is teaching that challenges are an opportunity for one's making and transformation and should therefore be embraced.

Chapter 7
Pathway to personal growth

Situation to address

Everyone for the most part wants to grow and develop as a person.

The question is "what's the most powerful pathway to this growth"?

Suggested mindset and approach

In a nutshell it's the <u>challenges and struggles</u> that one faces in life that, if approached in the right way, create the most phenomenal pathways to personal growth and self-development.

The most critical aspect is to accept and embrace these challenges with a positive mindset as, and when, they occur. Acknowledge that there will be many challenges in life, waiting for you ... there's no running away from them.

Trust that there's nothing like dealing with a challenge which enable you to discover and tap into previously unknown resources and capabilities.

Critical to your growth is accepting the challenge with absolute humility.

With this knowledge that untold personal growth and development will result from the process of dealing with the challenge, pursue it with confidence and perseverance.

Consciously make the most of how you can benefit from the challenges that come your way.

Results and benefits

Regardless of outcome, you will end up being a wiser, stronger and more capable person if you face each challenge positively.

Rather than feel bitter, or tell yourself "why me"…trust and know that you will learn about yourself - including a revelation of your personal resourcefulness.

Without question, others around you will be inspired by your resolve, strength and acceptance of the challenge at hand, making you a catalyst for growth and development of others too.

Impact takeaway

Your greatest and most impactful attributes are born from your greatest challenges.

Making it personal - consider:

1. When faced with a challenge - what is my immediate reaction… how have I dealt with them in the past?
2. Do I avoid dealing with a challenge or do I embrace it?
3. Is my mindset one of "this is only going to end with downside", or "I'm going to give it my best and know that, regardless, I will come out a better and stronger person".
4. How will I approach a challenge the next time one arises?

My role model "shout outs" who…

➢ "Achieved personal growth through challenges."

Insight from Torah Portion 8 – "Vayishlach"

Situation:

Esau, Jacob's twin brother, is approaching him with an army of 400 men to confront him and his family.

The conflict concerned Esau's wrongful claim that it was he, rather than Jacob, who was the rightful heir to the Jewish people.

Jacob, whilst being totally outnumbered by Esau, prepares for the inevitable confrontation in three ways:

- Sending messengers with gifts
- Prayer
- Preparing for battle

This preparation resulted in a peaceful and successful outcome:

Quote from the Torah:

Genesis 33:4 - "And Esau ran towards him (Jacob) and embraced him, and he fell on his neck and kissed him, and they wept"

Chassidic Insight:

When a situation of conflict and confrontation arises in life which requires to be dealt with, one needs to be proactive and resourceful.

Side stepping important causes of right and wrong is just not an option.

Chapter 8

Dealing with conflicts and confrontations

Situation to address

Regardless as to how uncomfortable it may feel, conflicts and confrontations happen in the workplace.

Question is, how should you approach them?

Suggested mindset and approach

To be clear, we are not considering small/minor matters, but rather those of principle.

Situations where you need to stand up for an important issue, be it personal or work related, because no one else can, and the consequences of not doing so would be highly detrimental.

There are three suggested steps:

1. Diffuse the conflict/confrontation
2. Internally reflect
3. Prepare for battle

<u>Diffusing a conflict</u> requires a wisely balanced overture to the "aggressor". Essentially, it means demonstrating sincere respect for the other party ahead of any meeting to "sort the matter out". Importantly, it does not mean accepting their position and essentially "rolling over", but rather, showing a gesture of friendship, whilst at the same time making it clear that you are resolved to "stand by your guns" and prepared to go head to head if need be. In this stage you are making it clear that you are grounded and determined in what you believe, but with a smile.

<u>Internal reflection</u> requires the attainment of absolute humility, which results in a stronger self-belief. It is a process to confirm that the conflict is not about your ego or hurt feelings (if it is then it's probably best to drop the issue), but rather on a fundamental matter of right or wrong, which is based upon a "bigger than me" issue. In this process of reflection, self-assurance, grounded confidence and clarity, as to what you are "fighting for", are the fruits and benefits of this step.

<u>Preparing for battle</u> essentially plans and maps out what happens if appeasement fails, and direct conflict can't be avoided. It involves developing strategies to minimise losses and know what you are prepared to sacrifice and lose, in the worst case scenario. Essentially here you are developing plans to fight smartly, and determinedly…. But most important of all, you are going to "battle" without ego or self-importance, but with true "higher" and meaningful purpose.

Results and benefits

The net result of this process is confidence and clarity.

It enables you to differentiate and identify what is really worth, or even relevant, to stand up to and go to battle for, and what is not. In fact, many times this process results in actually stepping down, and realizing the issue is just not worth a conflict.

It brings to light what is driven by ego and thus should be dropped, and what really is a cause worth escalating into conflict and confrontation for, and how to go about it.

Most important of all, it helps you to keep grounded, calm and collected in the process, maintaining your self-worth and dignity when dealing with matters of conflict, which absolutely need to be addressed.

Finally, the inspiration that you give others by taking on a conflict/confrontation which has a true higher purpose, and no ego, is truly impactful and should not be underestimated.

Impact takeaway

If necessary, be prepared to stand up for major causes of right and wrong for the greater good.

Making it personal - consider:

1. Have there been any major/important confrontational situations when it has been "on me" to take it on? (The answer to this could very well be no!)
2. If so, how did I deal with it? Did I have a clear view of the "higher" purpose?
3. Going forward, what advice would I give myself regarding steps to take, should a conflict/confrontation arise?
4. How would I approach appeasement, reflection and preparation for battle?

My role model "shout outs" who…

➢ "Stood up to conflicts constructively and purposely."

Insight from Torah Portion 9 – "Vayeishev"

Situation:

Joseph, (one of Jacob's 12 sons) is just 17 years old and has been unjustly thrown into prison in a foreign land far away from his family.

Despite his unfair, desperate and unfortunate position, he is not consumed with his own dire situation and misfortune.

Rather, he notices two of his fellow prisoners who seem troubled and asks them how they are.

They then reveal that each had some concerns on their minds which had just arisen from an intense dream the night before.

Joseph went on to interpret each one's dream. This later resulted in Joseph's release from prison.

Quote from the Torah:

Genesis 40:6-7 - "And Joseph came to them in the morning, and he saw them and behold, they were troubled… and he asked (them), "Why are your faces sad today?""

Chassidic Insight:

The two prisoners openly shared their problems because they sensed Joseph's genuine concern about their wellbeing.

This teaches us a powerful lesson, not to get self-absorbed in our own issues, but always keep an eye out for our fellow colleagues.

The consequences of such genuine concern can be life changing and hugely beneficial.

Chapter 9

Transform daily mundane interactions

Situation to address

Countless daily interactions, such as asking one another, "how are you?", are rarely expressed in a heartfelt or genuine way. For the most part these are mundane and thus wasted opportunities for meaningful engagement.

How can you transform everyday "niceties" into meaningful, high potential impact, events?

Suggested mindset and approach

The most important aspect is to *want* to hear the responses and develop a genuine sense of care and concern for others.

In addition to this you should not be self-absorbed in your own issues which may be present at the time.

With this "clean" undistracted mindset and *before* asking how they are, assess and observe for yourself whether the person seems to be having a "good day" or not… and only then, based on your assessment, genuinely ask them from a place of real interest, empathy and care.

Furthermore, with this more mindful approach, you may even find different vocabulary to engage with, other than the standard "how are you?", in order to encourage a genuine response.

Results and benefits

As a result of this genuine and undistracted approach, the delivery of "how are you" will have a different tone and sincerity, which from time to time, will stimulate and enhance the standard, reflexive "fine and you" reply.

Everyone knows that an absolutely "perfect" day is a relatively rare event. A genuine inquiry into how someone is really doing, can lead to a much needed sharing with a fellow human being (you) who is genuinely interested in listening.

Regardless, one thing is for sure, you will listen much more to how the answer is delivered, and from time to time a "real and honest" human exchange will occur.

This will result in a real connection with a fellow human being and, without question, will form a deeper relationship and level of trust than could otherwise occur.

This brief, honest, interaction creates, over time, a stronger trust and bond.

Taking just a minute or so to dialogue on a "human" interest, rather than purely work focused engagement, creates and enables a richer and more meaningful relationships, in work culture and environment.

There is a further bonus - this type of interaction tends to result in those individuals looking out for *your* best interest and be there for *you* when you need them.... Potentially bringing you untold personal benefits.

Impact takeaway

Asking "how are you?" is not a meaningless, hollow, cultural ritual but an invaluable opportunity to connect and build trusting connections and relationships.

Making it personal - consider:

1. When was the last time I asked someone at work how they were and really felt that I wanted to know the answer? Was there ever a time when I felt that 'something' wasn't right?
2. What was the response? Was it thoughtful and honest?
3. How did I feel about the exchange? Did I walk away with a stronger connection to the person? Do I think that they walked away with a stronger connection to me?

4. "How am I" going to approach asking people how they are, going forward?

My role model "shout outs" who…

➢ "Genuinely engage in day to day interactions."

Insight from Torah Portion 10 – "Miketz"

Situation

Pharaoh, the ruler of Egypt, has two dreams.

Previously we have been told of Joseph's two dreams. One involved him and his brothers, physically binding wheat, and the other dream depicted celestial images of the stars, moon and sun.

In Pharaoh's dreams, on the other hand, Pharaoh was just stationary, standing on a riverbank observing cows, and then stalks of grain.

Quote from the Torah:

Genesis 41:1-6 "Pharaoh was dreaming, and behold, he was standing by the Nile… And behold, from the Nile were coming up seven cows… and behold, seven ears of grain…"

Chassidic Insight:

What can be learnt from the difference between Joseph's and Pharaoh's dreams?

Dreams reflect one's intent and ambitions.

Joseph dreams of his direct physical efforts (in binding wheat) as well as a vision to reach for something beyond where he is currently, namely, to attain a higher purpose by reaching for the stars.

This compares to Pharaoh's dreams which had no active engagement as he was just a standing observer and only focussed on mundane, material, things - namely cows and grain. This inactive and material driven mindset reflected his own aspirations, namely material "inactive" pursuits.

From this we are warned not to make our 'dreams' or our goals about just making "easy money" with no personal effort.

Rather we should develop dreams and goals that have a higher ("stars, moon and sun") purpose, which require our active efforts, energy and engagement ("binding wheat").

Chapter 10

How to achieve your dreams

Situation to address

How to set one's sights for success.

Having an ultimate dream or vision of your personal ambition is critical to create an impact.

But how do you determine if it's the right vision and whether it will guide you to the right place?

Suggested mindset and approach

In summary, ask yourself, "What is my dream?"... then consider:

1. Do I have an active, meaningful, role in realising this dream, or am I just a bystander expecting others to fulfil it?
2. Is this a dream which I feel truly proud of and, objectively, which has a clear and positive impact with a higher purpose and benefit?

From your reflections on this, consider whether there will be a positive, broader impact to those around or is it just you who will be the main beneficiary?

Consider to what extent realizing your dreams is dependent on "luck", and how much is dependent on your own purposeful efforts and toil.

Reflect on how "luck" can be, or should be, disregarded in setting your dreams. This might require making more effort and/or perhaps refining the dream to be less dependent on luck.

Develop a mindset of continuously refining what your personal dreams mean to you, ensuring that achieving them will have a meaningful impact not only upon you but also upon those around you.

How can the boundaries of positive impact be stretched to the greater good?..., and, importantly, what can you, yourself, contribute in terms of time, skill and energy to realize the benefits of the "dream".

Remember the well-known expression – 'the harder I try, the luckier I get'.

Results and benefits

Typically, this approach results in a shift to a bigger, more impactful, "dream" which actually feels truer or more closely aligned to your skills.

Realizing a dream is also driven by factors which are under your control and direct efforts, rather than external factors or luck. As a result, the chances of realizing them are greater. In short – it's down to you!

Critically this also reflects a dream or a vision being less about "ego and self", and more about how you can have a broader, more sustainable, impact. Furthermore, the approach to realizing the dream becomes much more actionable and thus deliverable.

This, in turn, tends to result in greater levels of motivation, self-satisfaction and commitment to delivering your dream.

Essentially, this happens because you have developed a dream that is "bigger than you" and at the same time has limited ego attached to it.

Finally, the ultimate impact, or outcome, of the dream or vision tends to surpass and exceed any of your previous expectations.

Impact takeaway

Set actionable dreams that can bring widespread impact beyond "just me".... then actively make them happen.

Making it personal – consider:

1. What are my dreams?
2. Can I articulate the contribution required to realize my dreams? What more could I do?
3. Other than me, who else would benefit from the realization of my dreams?

4. Can I refine or change my dreams to make them more beneficial to more people and to a greater good?... If so, how?

My role model "shout outs" who...

➢ "Set and achieve ambitious goals for the greater good."

Insight from Torah Portion 11 – "Vayigash"

Situation:

Jacob has just been told that his cherished son Joseph, who had been missing for 20 years, presumed dead, is alive and well. Not only that, but he hears that Joseph has become very successful and is effectively running Egypt, the most powerful economy in the world.

However, on receiving the good news Jacob remains speechless, showing no reaction whatsoever.

Only upon hearing the complete message that, not only was Joseph successful but, importantly, he had maintained his personal values and standards, does Jacob speak, and says…

Quote from the Torah:

Genesis 45:28 "My son Joseph is still alive."

Chassidic Insight:

Why did Jacob remain silent when he initially heard that his beloved son Joseph was alive?

To be considered truly "alive", one must still maintain the highest of human standards and values, however successful one is in the material world.

To explain, Jacob knew that Egypt was a corrupt place. The news that his son was not only living there but running the country, was actually <u>devastating</u> news, as he presumed that he, Joseph, must have dropped his standards and values and adopted those of ancient Egypt.

As a result, based upon this initial news, Jacob could not consider Joseph to be truly "alive".

Only when Jacob was told, and understood, that in fact, Joseph had indeed <u>maintained and continued to uphold his righteousness</u> did he consider Joseph to be alive and part of humanity.

Chapter 11

Living according to your values

Situation to address

Achieving your dreams and realizing the fruits of success can adversely influence your ego.

How can you stay grounded and maintain your *essence* and *values,* especially while surrounded by the rewards of your achievements?

Suggested mindset and approach

Whilst in pursuit of your career, ambitions and goals, always be mindful of not compromising your basic "human" essence and values.

This way, even when success is realized, it does not come at the cost of compromising your standards and core values such as *honesty, integrity, respect, friendship* and *humility.*

Given the constant pressures to succeed, setting aside reflective time to consider your behaviours is invaluable.

Are there any aspects of your behaviour that you would be less than proud to share with others?

Consider maintaining a three monthly scorecard…. On one side, note your successes and achievements… and on the other side any adverse behaviours or actions you may have taken, which are below your personal standards.

Ask those closest to you if they have noticed any adverse changes.

In addition to this, consider your current/future goals, and note how you will not only maintain your personal core values and standards, but also how you will demonstrate them in an exemplar manner.

Results and benefits

A true measure of personal achievement can only be considered whilst maintaining, even enhancing, the quality and standards of your personal "human" values.

By not compromising who you are, despite achieving success, you are essentially setting yourself up for the next success.

Your team, colleagues and superiors will already be "on your side" and want you to succeed.

Demonstrating that success does not come at a personal "cost" but, rather, can lead to even more positive behaviours transforming and inspiring others to do the same.

Impact takeaway

Don't let achieving success "kill" the wonderful essence of who you are… rather, maintain your values and essence to deliver further impact.

Making it personal – consider:

1. What have my top three achievements in the workplace been?
2. How would I grade myself regarding my behaviours, standards and values, whilst achieving them?
3. Can I pinpoint any aspects of disappointment?
4. How could I approach my current goals whilst living according to my values?

My role model "shout outs" who…

➢ "Don't let fame and success change their qualities as a person."

Torah Insight from Portion 12 – "Vayechi"

Situation:

Before passing away, Jacob specifically blesses Joseph's two children. He wanted to bless them for their protection, as they were the first Jews who were born and lived outside the holy land of Israel, in a foreign culture.

On the surface he gives them a strange blessing:

Quote from the Torah:

Genesis 48:16 "May they multiply abundantly like fish.."

Chassidic Insight:

Why bless them as fish?

There are two critical aspects regarding fish.

1. *When you take a fish out of water it immediately becomes <u>aware</u> of the life threatening environment and does whatever it can to re-enter its normal habitat where it can live.*
2. *Fish are able to swim against the current.*

Both of these characteristics are critical to a fish's survival.

Wanting to get back into water is obvious to survival. The ability to swim upstream against the current, enables fish to find the right locations for their food and where to lay their eggs, and thereby thrive.

Developing an awareness of your environment, enables a conscious movement towards constructive rather than destructive surroundings.

This in turn develops strength of character to not blindly "follow the crowd" but rather to be true to yourself and be able to swim against the current if need be.

Consequently, Jacob's blessing was to ensure that his grandchildren, like fish, maintain an acute awareness of their environment and the ability to choose the right path, in order to always survive and thrive.

Chapter 12

Survive and thrive in any culture

Situation to address

How does one best "survive" any adverse cultural aspects which go against your values or preferences within the work rat race?

What does survival mean, what does it look like?

How can you even thrive within the rat race?

Suggested mindset and approach

The theme of being "true to yourself" whilst successfully pursuing your career and maximising your impact has been pondered for many years.

It continues to be relevant when considering how to best "survive" the process. More than this, survival also enables you to thrive.

Considering surviving and thriving in turn:

To survive:

Developing a clear awareness of the work culture and environment is critical.

In particular <u>identifying</u> and "labelling" any aspects which make you really uncomfortable; as it is these negative aspects that need to be specifically focused upon and addressed in order to "survive".

Consider how you can change, influence or avoid the aspects that you do not like, into something that would be more acceptable. Critically, we are not talking about ignoring or suppressing these aspects, as this will eventually only make you feel "crushed".

Consciously and purposefully develop strategies to make your environment one in which you feel comfortable. Achieve this and, in all probability, you will be able to "survive" your workplace.

<u>To thrive:</u>
The key to being able to thrive is to be comfortable not going with the flow/majority if you feel it's not right. (This is different from dealing with a major conflict which is covered in chapter 8).

Thriving is about taking the "risks" to express your opinions in a careful and considered manner and to do things that you think need to be done, as and when needed.

Importantly, this is not so much about doing things contrary to how things operate, but rather introducing new "ways" in how things can be done. To be able to bring people along with you on the journey and to be a positive influence in the workplace.

Essentially this involves behaving and expressing "who you are", so you can positively improve and contribute to the workplace. As a result of such an approach you not only survive but thrive within the workplace.

Results and benefits

By consciously going through this process, you begin to realize that you can change and improve your workplace environment and how it operates.

It is not just about putting up with the imperfections or aspects that make you feel bad, but rather to proactively deal with them.

Needless to say, you will feel a much stronger sense of belonging, as well as *self-worth*. This alone, can transform your contentment, wellbeing and general happiness not only in the workplace but at home too.

Finally, taking this conscious approach can facilitate you to create a "healthier" and better environment, better suited to you and your colleagues and, in turn, will enable you to thrive.

Impact takeaway

Knowing your core values and essence will enable you to proactively ensure how to survive and thrive within the workplace.

Making it personal – consider:

1. Are there any aspects within my work environment that make me feel really uncomfortable? If so, what are they?
2. How might I change or avoid these negative aspects?
3. Who else do I think shares my concerns? Can I perhaps collectively address them?
4. Are there any aspects within my workplace that should operate differently?
5. If so, how should I go about improving them?

My role model "shout outs" who…

➢ "Not swayed by an immoral majority."

Part II
Remove Limits To Your Potential

Insight from Torah Portion 13 – "Shemot"

Situation:

Jacob had previously been given the name Israel. He and all his family had moved to Egypt due to a famine. They were 70 strong in total when they arrived.

The family multiplied and expanded but were soon forced to become slaves to Pharaoh. This enslavement lasted for hundreds of years.

Despite living as slaves in the most powerful, foreign, materially driven country, amongst millions of other people, Jacob's family still maintained its own unique identity.

How was this accomplished?... The beginning of this period of enslavement, and the second of the five "books of Moses" starts with:

Quote from the Torah:

Exodus 1:1 "And these are the <u>names</u> of the sons of Israel.."

Chassidic Insight:

Why does the Torah begin describing the enslavement of the people in Egypt by <u>repeating</u> the names of Israel… a fact that was already known?

From this we learn that in order <u>not</u> to become enslaved and lose one's own unique identity within a powerful and dominant (material) environment we need to remind ourselves as to who we truly are.

This is emphasised by the repetition and reminder of their unique names. In fact, despite enslavement, the people of Israel kept their Hebrew names - they did not adopt Egyptian ones.

Chassidic philosophy teaches that one's name reflects the true essence of your soul and being. By having your soul's unique essence in mind, as a result of keeping to Hebrew names, you can never become permanently enslaved, or lost to an all-encompassing powerful environment. As a result, the people retained the freedom to live life in a way which is true to their higher essence and purpose.

Chapter 13

Work to live, rather than live to work

Situation to address

The question "What do you do for a living?", all too often results in a response that describes one's work/career.

Why has this become a common response, rather than truly answering the question regarding what "living", and thus what life mean to you?

If you are not careful, your work and work environment can totally take over your life to the point that all you do is think of, and associate, every aspect of life to work, thereby losing yourself… forgetting who you are and totally associating your identity and life focus with your work.

How can this be avoided and best managed?

Suggested mindset and approach

This general and widespread desensitisation to work taking over your life is the key driving force behind this book which this section will begin to address.

At the heart of avoiding the trap of living your life as if it was only about work, you should simply focus and remind yourself of who you really are.

Start with *your* individual identity. Who are you? How would your loved ones describe you as a person? What do people like about you? How have you recently helped someone in need or shown kindness?

The answers to these and other similar questions reflect who you really are and, in fact, what you *really* do for a living. For sure these aspects can be experienced inside as well as outside work, however they also fall outside your "work".

Consider what your "job titles" or labels are, outside work:- parent, friend, child, carer, youth leader, mentor, team member or volunteer? Or, more likely, a combination of these roles.

All these roles clearly have an important impact in life, which goes way beyond the workplace.

Regular reminders that give a broader perspective as to who you really are and what your life is about will help balance what your life is really about.

Results and benefits

As a result of this approach, no matter how absorbed you might be at the workplace, you will still maintain a true feeling of self-worth, which reaches beyond the workplace and your work.

This reduces the risk of being totally consumed with your work/career and helps maintain a broader and healthier perspective to life.

In short you will be more aligned with your core essence and who you are. Critically, you will not feel enslaved by your career and your work, as you will have an acute awareness and reminder as to how you can positively influence the world outside the workplace…This is an invaluable aspect as to who you are and what your life is about.

Furthermore, when work perhaps doesn't go so well, or even if you lose your job, this has a far less negative impact on you, because you have become far more resilient. Your self-worth is not defined to such a great extent by your work, and you are therefore far better equipped to respond and deal with challenges.

Importantly, you also become less dependent on work which, invariably, for most of us, is somewhat out of the realms of our control, particularly earlier in our careers, and thereby we tend to feel less anxious about its inevitable uncertainties.

Impact takeaway

My life is far more than my career!

Making it personal – consider:

1. How would my loved ones describe me as a person? What do people like about me? How have I recently helped someone in need or shown kindness?
2. What are my "job titles" or labels outside work? Who benefits from me taking on these roles?
3. What do I truly live for?
4. What would I like to be remembered for, and what am I doing about it?
5. What would my answer be if someone asked me "What do you do for a living?"

My role model "shout outs" who…

➢ "Works to live, not lives to work."

Insight from Torah Portion 14 – "Va'era"

Situation:
Moses has been chosen by God to lead the children of Israel out of slavery after hundreds of years in Egypt. He feels totally daunted by this task, especially how he could even approach Pharaoh, the ruler of Egypt regarding this.

Quote from the Torah:
Exodus 6:13: Moses spoke before the Lord, saying "….How then will Pharaoh hearken to me, seeing that I am of <u>closed lips</u>?"

Chassidic Insight:
Moses was ultimately successful in liberating the people. But what was the connection between his ultimate success and him feeling so helpless at the outset?

Had Moses felt that he did, in fact, have the necessary skills, in many ways his approach would have been limited by his own personal view of his capabilities.

But feeling that he had no capability whatsoever, even to the extent that he couldn't speak with Pharaoh, enabled him to dig deeper, enabling himself to go beyond his limiting beliefs and tap into his essence.

The combination of his humility together with a determined approach to save his people, brought to the surface the qualities for which he was chosen to do the job.

Chapter 14

Delivering the (apparent) impossible

Situation to address

You've been selected to take on a significant new responsibility, promotion or task which makes you feel totally daunted and out of your depth.

How can you tap into those hidden capabilities which others believe you have?

Suggested mindset and approach

It is completely natural that you will own and acknowledge your feelings of uncertainty and even anxiety, in taking on this new challenge and responsibility.

In many ways this "ownership and acknowledgement" is at the core of the suggested approach.

Establish a sense of reassurance and confidence in those who choose you, and their rationale and judgement in wanting you. They are obviously seeing potential and untapped strengths within you that you are not fully aware of.

Grab this opportunity to learn and discover more about who you are, rather than walk away and never really get to know the extent of your gifts.

By all means, question and challenge their choice and belief in you, if you wish to, but essentially transform your doubt into a sense of humility combined with selfless determination to be successful.

Results and benefits

This approach will facilitate bringing out the, as of yet, untapped resources within you, and in effect it will reveal to yourself more of your essence and the hidden potential that exists within you.

Whilst you might not perform the task "perfectly" at first, without doubt the experience will enable you to understand your true capabilities and the extent of what you are able to offer.

Not only will the previous, seemingly "impossible" task be delivered, but in addition to this, a whole new "universe" of potential opportunities and achievements will open up to you, which previously appeared out of reach.

Impact takeaway

Raise your glass ceiling. You are more capable than you think you are. What might feel like a mission impossible, can reveal the hidden potential that you possess.

Making it personal – consider:

1. Have I ever been given a "mission impossible"? What did I do? How did I feel?
2. How would I approach it next time round?
3. Do I sometimes receive feedback that I feel is better than I deserve?
4. How can I reveal within myself the untapped potential that others see?

My role model "shout outs" who…

> "Break through limiting personal beliefs."

Insight from Torah Portion 15 – "Bo"

Situation:
The children of Israel have just attained freedom after being enslaved in Egypt for hundreds of years. As they leave, they take unleavened dough with them.

Quote from the Torah:
Exodus 12:39 "They baked the dough that they had taken out of Egypt as unleavened cakes, for it had not leavened"

Chassidic Insight:
What's the connection between unleavened dough and a newfound freedom?

Egypt was a country obsessed with materialism and ruled by a culture driven by self-importance and ego (Pharaoh himself claimed to be god and creator of the river Nile, which was Egypt's key source of wealth). The Hebrew word for Egypt also means restrained/held back.

From this we are taught that any desires or emotions that come from a place of ego, end up enslaving you and holding you back in life.

Unleavened bread, in contrast, has no air or "puff" in it (as it has not yet fermented). As a result, it is flat.

Being full of "puff and air" relates to being full of ego and self-importance. This can reveal itself in several ways, from being caught up in material desires to negative emotions.

Whereas being unleavened, with no air, reflects a state of humility and self-nullification.

It is this sense of humility that enables you to attain true personal freedom from being entrapped by your ego.

Chapter 15
Feel free to be who you are

Situation to address

Is there anything holding you back from your true potential?

Are you being distracted by personal worries, desires or motives?

How can you release yourself to be free to be the "real" you and achieve your true potential?

Suggested mindset and approach

Consider what is holding you back in life.

Identify the "unhealthy"/negative thoughts and emotions which are consuming you in the workplace. Essentially, these tend to come from the ego and falsely placed expectations such as:

- Materialism/money obsessions and desires
- Jealousy
- Insecurities
- Fear of failure
- Worrying about what people think of you
- Trying to please others in order to be accepted
- Having negative feelings towards colleagues
- Disappointment
- Anger/frustration

These thoughts do nothing to truly benefit you in the workplace. In fact, these ego driven emotions invariably block and hold you back from achieving your true potential.

The best way to deal with them is to just ignore them and clear them out of your mind.

Whilst this is easier said than done, by developing an awareness as to what they are, when you identify and become conscious of such negative thoughts, then try not to dwell on them. Instead, try to ignore them.

In their place, adopt a mindset which is not based on "self-centred thoughts, expectations or beliefs", but rather, humble acceptance and gratitude for all situations.

Realize that restraining thoughts and limiting beliefs are driven by ego. Freedom to be the best you, comes from humility.

Results and benefits

The combination of having the strength of mind to identify and ignore negative "restraining" thoughts, results in a powerful sense of true freedom to "be you" in the workplace.

This will free you to clearly see and then unreservedly deal with the situations at hand, unencumbered by any other factors, in an objective, grounded and impactful way.

Your potential essence will thereby be unleashed, as it is not being held back by false, ego driven, beliefs or thoughts.

Needless to say, your impact in the workplace will be transformational.

Colleagues will sense your clear thinking and humble approach to levering your strengths.

Without question this will have a positive and influential impact upon the people you engage with at work, be it team colleagues, customers or other related parties.

Impact takeaway

Leave your ego,… free and unleash your potential through humility, acceptance and gratitude.

Making it personal – consider:

1. What are my negative thoughts and emotions in the workplace?
2. Can I identify how they come from a place of ego?
3. How can I train myself to ignore them?
4. How can I adopt a more humble mindset which is not based on "self-expectations", but rather acceptance and gratitude?
5. What are my strengths compared to others at work? Do I view them as gifts?
6. How might others use such similar gifts better than I am currently doing?

My role model "shout outs" who…

➢ "Has no ego."

Insight from Torah Portion 16 – "Beshalach"

Situation:

On leaving Egypt the people of Israel are attacked by two nations, Egypt and Amalek. Regarding the Egyptian army, the people of Israel are told by God to ignore them and keep moving forward. Regarding Amalek, they are told to attack.

Quote from the Torah:

Exodus 17:9 "So Moses said to Joshua, pick men for us, and go out and fight against Amalek."

Chassidic Insight:

Why did God command the people of Israel to attack Amalek on the one hand and to ignore the battle overtures from Egypt on the other?

Egypt represents ego and a desire for materialism. Such feelings should just be ignored.

For Amalek, however, a different approach was needed, as they wanted to create self-doubt within Israel.

The people of Amalek knew that considering all the open miracles that had happened to the people of Israel, there was no way that they could beat them in battle. Their mindset, however, was to "cool down" the enthusiasm and confidence that Israel was feeling at the time. With continuous battles, over time their hope was to create doubt in Israel's confidence, enough so that they no longer felt the commitment they once had, with the hope that eventually Amalek could overcome them.

Furthermore, the numerical equivalent of the Hebrew word Amalek (as each letter has a number associated with it), is the same as "sofek", which means doubt. This doubt had to be attacked head on and erased, unlike ego, which could just be ignored.

Consequently, we can learn from this that whenever we have any doubt, coolness, or loss of enthusiasm, with regards an aspect or goal in life which is critical, you should fight any such negative feelings head on, to crush and eradicate them.

Chapter 16
Dealing with loss of enthusiasm

Situation to address

Ambitious long-term goals, and plans to deliver them, have been set.

You know what needs to be done and were once excited, but then self-doubt creeps in and enthusiasm wanes.

How should this be dealt with?

Suggested mindset and approach

In summary, consciously crush and wipe out any such feelings.

Many important business goals (personal or organizational), whether a project, event or target, take time to deliver. Whilst the importance of each goal remains, your enthusiasm and drive may wane over time.

As a result, your commitment to achieve it might reduce, resulting in total, or partial, failure to deliver.

This may be due to feeling overwhelmed, doubting the importance of the goal, or your ability to deliver it.

This doubt may arise from a feeling of "coolness" and reduced internal drive to achieve the goal, or even self-doubt, thus reducing the confidence you once had.

The key is to be aware of your feelings towards the goal in question, and, rather than ignoring such feelings, purposefully "crush" them internally by reminding yourself of the goal, its importance, and your determination and capability to deliver on it.

Furthermore, regular team meetings and discussions with trusted colleagues can be set to prod and bolster all relevant people, reminding them of their commitment and the importance of delivering the set goal.

Results and benefits

This approach, of "crushing and wiping out" any cooling off in one's enthusiasm to achieve a long-term goal, will help turn the tide. It often happens in many organizations that major initiatives, on launch, create a huge buzz, excitement and commitment, but eventually fizzle out.

This approach will result in more major goals being delivered which, in turn, breeds a "can do" culture, with determined perseverance to deliver more ambitious goals.

With the right approach, culture will not just "eat strategy for breakfast", but rather will deliver the strategy beyond expectations and exceed previous track records.

Impact takeaway

Crushing doubt and keeping enthusiasm high is a game changer to delivering long-term ambitious goals.

Making it personal – consider:

1. How has my personal enthusiasm and drive waned over time when engaging in delivering a long-term goal?
2. What could I have done differently to maintain high levels of enthusiasm, commitment and drive?
3. Going forward how could I adopt techniques to ensure sustainable higher levels of drive, self-belief and commitment to deliver?

My role model "shout outs" who…

➢ "Never let enthusiasm wane in delivering long-term goals."

Insight from Torah Portion 17 – "Yitro"

Situation:

Having just left Egypt and defeated their enemies, the people of Israel become dependent on Moses every time they have a question. Moses' father-in-law comments how this situation is untenable.

Quote from the Torah:

- *Exodus 18:17-18, "Moses' father-in-law said to him, "The thing you are doing is not good. You will surely wear yourself out both you and these people. You cannot do it alone."*
- *Exodus 18:21, "But you shall choose out of the entire nation people of substance, God fearers, people of truth who hate monetary gain, and you shall appoint over them [Israel] leaders over thousands, ... hundreds, ...fifties, and .. tens."*
- *Exodus 18:22, "And they shall judge the people at all times, and it shall be that any <u>major</u> matter they shall bring to you."*
- *Exodus 18:23, "If you do this thing, and the Lord commands you, you will be able to survive and also, all this people will come upon their place in peace."*
- *Exodus 18 24-26, "Moses obeyed his father-in-law... the <u>difficult</u> cases they would bring to Moses".*

Chassidic Insight:

Notwithstanding how wise and awesome a leader is, a process of delegation is critical for the "survival, success and impact" of both the leader and the people that he leads. Defining "major" and "difficult" matters appropriately, is critical. The only change Moses made to the advice given, was to have the difficult and complex matters come to him. Straight forward matters, even if large, were not brought to him.

The selection of people to whom authority is given, is drawn from already successful, proven, capable people who have a combination of humility, honesty and an absence of ego. Thus, the toughest and most complex matters are passed up the chain, to the point where the most appropriate and capable person is able to deal with it.

Chapter 17

Delegation: mastering a double edged sword

Situation to address

Without appropriate delegation things would grind to a halt due to an overload on key people, especially at the top of the organization.

In addition, misdirected delegation can result in damaging and adverse outcomes due to authority being given to the wrong people.

The question is, how can you reach the right "delegation" balance?

Suggested mindset and approach

Good delegation firstly requires a deep appreciation of its importance and impact, so that it is a prioritized aspect of work – important to "get right".

Essentially, the mindset of someone in a leadership position, should be to delegate "everything", with only the toughest, most complex aspects coming to him.

In addition to this, is a conscious contemplation of two key factors, namely:

i. <u>Understanding</u> the tasks – the hierarchy of what the hardest, most complex, highest risk tasks are, down to the most straight forward and simple ones.
ii. <u>Understanding</u> the people – the strengths, characters and capabilities of the people around you, who would take the additional authority and responsibly without ego.

By applying these two steps, tasks are confidently delegated, essentially matching tasks to those whose skills most aptly complement the degree of complexity, experience and expertise required.

It is of critical importance to not confuse the size of the task or the decision, with the complexity and risk associated with getting it done right.

Results and benefits
A leader who is mindful to "delegate as much as possible" is rewarded with the most precious of gifts, namely, more time to create more impact.

Benefits of effective delegation also include:
- Bandwidth to establish high, value generating, strategies, enabling the organization to progress more successfully.
- Time for leaders to build the best and strongest teams
- Effective, focused, execution of key activities
- High quality output - having the right people doing the right tasks
- Lower costs, especially in the area of highly skilled labour, as utilization is optimized
- Higher job satisfaction from greater and more appropriate allocation of tasks, matched with skills
- Lower stress and anxiety by having the right people doing what is within their skill set
- Optimizing skills most needed to be recruited, as well as cost cutting opportunities where there is an excess of (expensive) skills
- Enabling a more agile and flexible culture to respond to new opportunities and challenges
- Increasing the organization's short and long-term success

Impact takeaway
Delegation enables *everyone* to be a winner and frees the organization from being unnecessarily held back.

Making it personal – consider:
1. How effective is my delegation?
2. Do I have enough time to think about the important, complex, matters and set my best vision and ambition?

3. Do I feel that I'm always doing too much?
4. How much better would I feel if I delegated more responsibility to others?
5. Am I worried by loss of control? How can I mitigate this risk by spending more time carefully selecting, building, developing and if needed, recruiting appropriate skills?

My role model "shout outs" who…

➤ "Masters delegation of what, to who and when."

Insight from Torah Portion 18 – "Mishpatim"

Situation:

God has just spoken to <u>all</u> the people of Israel for the first time and given them the Ten Commandments. This momentous event officially started the process of conveying "the word of God", namely the book of the Torah, containing Divine lessons and a guide to life (as well as all 613 commandments for the Jewish people to adhere to).

The first lesson conveyed after this momentous event is about slavery and how to treat servants.

Quote from the Torah:

Exodus 21:1-2: "And these are the rulings that you shall set before them. Should you buy a slave…."

Chassidic Insight:

At this momentous moment of receiving the Ten Commandments, of all teachings, why start with a lesson about slavery? After all, given hundreds of years in slavery in Egypt, weren't the Israelites already experts in slavery and, more importantly, in how to treat them properly? What more could there be to learn?

Even in aspects of life where you consider yourself to be an expert, the most important mindset is to acknowledge how little you know, certainly so compared to God's Infinite Wisdom.

As such, you need to explore new initiatives and insights to further expand your capabilities and set new frontiers well beyond current limitations.

Thus, the Torah is teaching us that no matter how expert you might be there is always more to learn and different ways to further develop and grow. Moreover, this approach to areas of expertise is critical to a nations' (and an individual's) ability to thrive and continue to develop and progress.

For all these reasons, this was the first lesson that needed to be taught.

Chapter 18

What to do once you become an 'expert'

Situation to address

As your career develops, you could, or may even already have, improved an expertise in a certain aspect of work. You may even be the best in what you do.

So, what now?

Suggested mindset and approach

Whilst being expert in something it is important to recognise and, if need be, convince yourself, that you absolutely do not know it all but, rather, you have just scratched the surface.

Realize that if you're not determined to keep learning and developing, your relative level of expertise could diminish, thus reducing your impact and potential contribution. Look at your skill and ability from a whole different perspective and vision. Set yourself new frontiers in applying your skill, and how you can further develop and build upon your existing capabilities.

Critical to this thought process is to think just how much more benefit, positivity, and good can be achieved by what you do.

Essentially, there is always room to developand become better at what you do. Key to this is to keep an open mind and a determination to learn more. In this rapidly changing world you need to keep up with changing trends otherwise your skill set will gradually become redundant.

Results and benefits

This mindset can revolutionize, reinvent, and create new ways and approaches to do whatever it is you're expert at.

It enables you to always keep a fresh but nonetheless humble perspective, despite still performing tasks to a high standard.

High engagement and low boredom is another big win for anyone who is able to master the skill of "knowing everything" but yet realizing you know very little.

In fact, many highly successful corporations continue to thrive, develop and grow decade upon decade, primarily because their underlying character/culture is to never rest on their laurels in terms of where they are or how they view the market potential.

Rather, they continuously push the boundaries. Driving this requires a team of people who have a similar mindset in how they view themselves, and in setting their own personal individual ambitions, visions and new boundaries.

By not adopting this approach you could eventually become marginalized or redundant – how many lamp lighters or chimney sweeps are there left in the world today!

You either go forward or you go backward. There is no such thing as standing still.

Impact takeaway

There's always more to know and learn, especially if it's something you excel at.

Making it personal – consider:

1. What do I and others think I am great at?
2. How long has this been the case?
3. What am I doing about reinventing how I perform, to revolutionize my capability?
4. How could the brilliance of what I do be eclipsed by something or someone else?

5. What can I do about it?
6. Ask yourself "Am I going forward or, in fact, am I going backward?"

My role model "shout outs" who…

➢ "Always pushes personal boundaries of excellence."

Insight from Torah Portion 19 – "Terumah"

Situation:
Having successfully escaped from Egypt, the people of Israel are asked to make contributions to build a holy Sanctuary.

Quote from the Torah:
Exodus 25:2 "Speak to the children of Israel and have them <u>take</u> for Me an offering; from <u>every</u> person whose heart inspires him to generosity".

Chassidic Insight:
Why is the word "take" used? We would have expected the Torah to have used "give".

The word "take" rather than "give" is used to emphasize that everything we have in life is a gift from God. Thus, the command was to "take" from these gifts which each individual had received.

This implies a certain humility and appreciation of the gifts with which you have been blessed, and therefore an <u>obligation</u> to share them for the benefit of the world.

Furthermore '<u>every</u> person whose heart inspires him', implies that each person has a <u>unique</u> set of gifts from which you are able make a <u>unique</u> donation and contribution to the world.

From this we learn that each of us has something unique and special which we can contribute, towards the benefit of all.

Thus, <u>taking</u> from your unique God given gifts, implies your unique impact is something that no one else could ever make… and should you choose not to do it, the world would miss out from this gift.

Chapter 19

How to approach using your unique gifts

Situation to address

Everyone has unique God given gifts.

How should you approach using them?

How can you ensure that your gifts are used to the optimum benefit?

Suggested mindset and approach

On the surface, whilst it may not sound to be the intuitive answer, you need to adopt a "taker" rather than "giver" mindset.

Essentially you need to acknowledge that your strengths and gifts are gifted to you. If you like, you are born with them.

So, whilst you may build on these gifts and nurture them, you should always remind yourself that your gifts are given to you by God and you should consider yourself lucky/fortunate <u>recipients</u> of these gifts.

This approach creates a mindset of humility, obligation and personal responsibility.

As a result, the critical approach and attitude is to "<u>take</u>" from the gifts that you have been uniquely blessed with, and seek to share them as extensively as possible.

This ability to "take" from the gifts that you have been given, can be greatly enhanced by realizing that your gifts are absolutely unique.

This is because no one else will have the same mix and combination of *your* gifts, and thus only *you* can bring this unique combination of gifts into the world.

Consequently, should you not be able to optimize the use of your gifts, no one else is capable of filling the vacuum.

Taking from your gifts implies an obligation or responsibility which cannot be donated by anyone other than you.

Results and benefits

This personal acknowledgement and reflection will reduce any egotistical approaches to using these gifts, thereby avoiding a "look how good I am", or "I'm doing you a favour" attitude.

Rather, you will be more mindful to feel the responsibility and obligation to utilize and share the gifts, and thereby the impact that you can make is significantly enhanced.

Consequently, you become more motivated to "dig deeper", to ensure that your unique gifts are brought out and utilized to your best ability.

Without question, this also brings about a healthy feeling of self-worth and purpose in life.

Impact takeaway

A determined approach of "taking" from your gifts brings about a unique and positive impact that otherwise would never materialize.

Making it personal – consider:

1. What are my unique gifts and strengths that I have been fortunate to receive?
2. How do I use them with a sense of purpose?
3. What additional steps could be taken to enhance how my gifts are currently put to best use?
4. How can I take from my gifts and sense my personal obligation and responsibility to use them with humility?

My role model "shout outs" who…

- "Uses their gifts for the benefit of others."

Insight from Torah Portion 20 – "Tetzaveh"

Situation:

Whilst many materials were used for the Sanctuary, particular focus was given to the making of the olive oil, which was used as the fuel to generate light.

Quote from the Torah:

Exodus 27:20 "And you (i.e. Moses) shall command (Tetzaveh) the children of Israel, and they shall take to you pure olive oil, pressed for lighting, to kindle the lamps continually."

Chassidic Insight:

Why is Moses doing the "commanding" rather than God? And why specifically regarding the making of the oil for lighting?

For the first time, Moses, the **leader** of the people, is told to <u>actually give the command</u>, rather than just communicate the command given by God. The command related to the making of the olive oil used for lighting the Menorah and brings many insights regarding the role of a leader, including:

- The Hebrew word for command (Tetzaveh) also means to "connect". Hence the role of a leader is to connect with the people.

- Through this connection, a leader has the opportunity to reveal the "source of light" (represented by the oil), **within each individual**, **to that individual**, by applying the right pressure (<u>pressed</u> for lighting).

- The individual keys in to their unique light/skills through this connection with the leader, and is thereby able to bring out a light and tap in to positive energy which otherwise would not have been apparent.

- This source of light is then brought to the leader, ("take to you") and, in fact, increases the light which the leader would not otherwise be able to generate on their own.

Chapter 20

Revealing the potential in others

Situation to address

We all have a key responsibility of bringing the best out of people.

However, how can this be achieved? What approach should be used?

What can I do whether I'm an official leader or just a colleague?

Suggested mindset and approach

Whether you are the official leader or not, you can still take the lead and initiative in revealing the potential in others.

There are three key steps. The first is to take the time and effort to connect and understand the "magic" that exists within each individual.

This critical step requires you to pause and get to know and connect with each individual in a genuine, humble and insightful way, rather than just focusing on "giving out the orders".

The second step requires you to ensure the individual can recognise their true, unique, strengths. This might require some "pressure" to be applied, in order to convince and reveal to them their inherent strengths.

Finally, with the benefit of this internal confidence and self-worth, revealed within each individual, you need to ensure that the individual then ultimately utilizes their unique "oil", transforming it into "light" to benefit the workplace.

So, in summary, by genuinely connecting with individuals, a leader (or even a colleague) is able to see and understand what makes that individual so special and thereby enables them to discover and then use their essential gifts.

Results and benefits

Mastering this process is likely to unlock one of the most impactful aspects of leadership - releasing each individual's unique potential to contribute to the workplace.

There is an unquestionable transformation in people's output as they recognise and acknowledge their strengths and unique potential. This increase in output is driven by an internal confidence and a humble, yet determined, sense of purpose and sense of duty to utilize their unique strengths.

Because these insights are revealed through the trusted and wise mentoring and guidance of their "leader", individuals in turn become determined to utilize their strengths for the benefit of their leader's overall goals and objectives.

Essentially, this approach of investing time to understand the essence of individuals, results in a huge "win / win" for individuals, leaders and, of course, the entire organization.

This approach also brings to light the *all too frequent* mistake and misconception of many leaders who do not seem to understand what true leadership is.

Many confuse the primary focus of leadership with making decisions and setting direction. Bringing the best out of the people, results in achieving high goals, as well as, ultimately, the best decisions being taken. This is considered in greater depth within Part IV of this book.

Impact takeaway

The single most important priority for a leader is to ensure the potential and unique light within every person is recognized by that person and then utilized to its maximum potential.

Making it personal – consider:

1. How can I make time to really understand the unique essence of each individual in my team?
2. To what extent can I confidently describe each individual's unique strengths?

3. How can I make sure they understand what's so special about them?
4. How often will I remind them about their unique strengths?
5. To what extent is each person confident in, and actually using, their unique strengths?

My role model "shout outs" who…

➢ "Enables others to see their own uniqueness and qualities."

Insight from Torah Portion 21 – "Ki Tisa"

Situation:

The people of Israel are counted for the first time. The method of counting them is now described. Namely, each person is required to give a half silver Shekel coin, the coins are then counted, and the final sum determines how many people there were.

Quote from the Torah:

Exodus 30:12-13 "When you take the sum of the children of Israel according to their numbers, …. This they shall give, everyone who goes through the counting: half a Shekel"

Chassidic Insight:

Why is only half a Shekel used, why not a whole?

Half a Shekel rather than a whole, indicates that each individual cannot consider themselves to be complete.

Consequently, we are reminded that we all rely on others in order to achieve our potential.

Also, interestingly, each person donated the same value, implying that from God's perspective there was a certain equality amongst the people.

In addition to this, we later learn that the silver collected was melted and used to make the silver bases and clasps that held up the Sanctuary.

Extraordinarily, the exact amount of silver required for this was collected.

From this we understand that if just one person was missing, the whole structure would have been weaker. This reminds us that <u>everyone</u> counts, everyone has an important role to play.

Chapter 21

Fact: You can't do it by yourself. So How?

Situation to address

How can I get the best out of me?

Is my success all down to me, or do I need others?

Suggested mindset and approach

At the heart of this mindset, each individual needs to know and understand two critical aspects.

The <u>first</u> is to realize and appreciate that in order to achieve one's potential, every person is dependent on connecting with others, and that no one has what it takes to achieve their best by themselves.

This reality applies to every individual who has ever achieved anything significant. Namely, that there has always been some dependency on others, regardless as to whether the input was large or small.

Consequently, everyone should carefully consider who can provide help and support to them in respect of each challenge, be it from advice to actual help with that particular challenge.

<u>Secondly</u>, to develop a profound appreciation that everyone has a unique contribution to make and, should that contribution be missing, this would result in an unfulfilled piece of potential.

Essentially, every single human being counts and because of this gift of life, were any individual to be missing, then the whole of humanity would be lacking a piece of the puzzle of creation, and therefore be weaker as a result.

Results and benefits

Reality, realization and recognition that collective strength, mutual appreciation and respect is critical to ensuring that you are able to not only realize your own potential but also to enable the entire collective group to achieve its optimum impact.

All too often people are mistaken by thinking that there is conflict between getting the best out of themselves and getting the best out of the team.

In fact, the sooner one realizes that the two are in fact complementary and working in tandem, the sooner and faster the potential is realized, as well as that of the overall success of the organization.

As the old adage goes, thin sticks can be broken one at a time, but bind them together, and they are exponentially stronger.

Impact takeaway

Connecting with, and appreciating "you", enables a better "me". The whole is so much more than the sum of the parts.

Making it personal – consider:

1. Do I reach out enough to seek the help and support of others? What more should I do?
2. Where are my weak spots that need to be resolved? Who can help with these?
3. How can I appreciate that, at the end of the day, "we all come from dust and end up as dust", and have the same life force within us?
4. How can I better understand that everyone collectively makes the organization what it is and that if anyone is missing then we are all impacted?

My role model "shout outs" who…

➢ "Works with others to get best collective results."

Insight from Torah Portion 22 – "Vayakel"

Situation:
The building of the holy Sanctuary now takes place, and individuals are selected for this honoured task. Each one of them needed to have a very specific attribute:

Quote from the Torah:
Exodus 35:10 "Let all of <u>wise heart</u> amongst you come and do…"

Chassidic Insight:
Why is the attribute of a "wise heart" required to build the Sanctuary? What, in fact, is a wise heart?

The description, "wise heart" (rather than the more typical, "wise head" or "emotional heart"), is used, as it represents someone who, through their <u>mind and thoughts, is in control of their emotions</u>.

Wisdom is of no use unless expressed using the right constructive emotion.

Likewise, emotions, if mindlessly applied, can cause damage through ego driven behaviours rather than from a place of emotional intelligence.

As a result, for the best outcome, especially for the critical missions of building the holy Sanctuary, a wise heart is no contradiction but rather, the necessary combination.

Thus, in selecting a team of people for an important task, one should ensure they <u>first</u> have the "know how" (wisdom) and <u>then</u> the aligned emotional approach (heart) to fulfil that important task.

Chapter 22

Is it better to be a thinker or a feeler?

Situation to address

What is the key attribute of a good team player?

Thinker or feeler?

Suggested mindset and approach

In summary, ideally it is best to ensure each team member has both. The know how/intellectual capability, as well as the emotional skills to fulfil the task.

Thus, selecting individuals with both thinking and feeling capabilities is key.

As individuals tend to have one strength or another, efforts should be made to develop the weaker attribute of each individual - be it thinking or feeling.

Importantly, thinking (mindfulness) needs to come before feelings (heart and emotions), as your mind needs to control your heart and emotions.

Starting with the mind enables appreciation of the responsibility and opportunity, or potential impact, of the task or job at hand, leading to being "mindful" about the most appropriate feelings or emotions most suitable or aligned, for the task.

Emotions or feelings fall into seven categories (according to Torah), namely:
- Love and joy for the task
- Discipline required
- Empathy, compassion to enable a "beautiful" and balanced outcome
- Ambition

- Humility
- Connections with people
- Pride in getting the job done/outcome

Essentially, an element of all these emotions/feelings will be required, but depending on the situation, some more than others.

Results and benefits

By having a thoughtful and mindful approach to your work, the ultimate goal is always kept in mind and therefore appropriately actioned and implemented.

Combining the two aspects, wisdom directs feelings and emotions of the heart in a constructive, balanced and inclusive way, for the good of the desired goal/outcome.

A mindful and emotional approach enables irrelevant or even frivolous feelings or emotions to be quickly "noticed" and dropped. This, in turn, allows more responsible and appropriate emotions to be adopted.

More importantly, "keeping check" on how you should feel about the task or job enables you to behave with little or no ego, thereby optimizing the necessary behaviours to achieve it.

Your actions, speech and even thought process in completing the work will be harnessed in the most impactful way, which will not only result in a far better, indeed maybe the best outcome, but also inspire others who witness the behaviours adopted.

Whilst this is all "easier said than done", with continuous practise and effort, you can become highly skilled in mastering your feelings and emotions in the workplace which, in turn, will have transformational impacts.

Impact takeaway

"Mind & heart harmony" is a game changer to outcomes and results.

Making it personal – consider:

1. To what extent am I aware of my emotions when at work?

2. How can I actively connect my understanding of the task with how I behave?
3. Are there any examples in which I or others have thoughtfully approached a task in an inspiring and transformative way? What were the emotions being adopted?
4. How can I make this approach second nature?

My role model "shout outs" who…

➢ "Combine both smart thinking and constructive emotional engagement."

Insight from Torah Portion 23 – "Pekudei"

Situation:

Donations of materials for the Sanctuary have been completed.

Moses now commands that all materials (gold, silver, precious gems and other items) with which he was entrusted, was to be accounted for.

Quote from the Torah:

Exodus 38:21 "These are the accounts of the Sanctuary ... which were accounted at Moses' command".

Chassidic Insight:

All commands normally came from God to Moses who then, in turn, communicated God's command to the people.

Why was this command directly from Moses?

By taking the initiative himself, he set the tone and demonstrated as leader of the people the importance of integrity and transparency.

Moses was not only able to build undisputed trust with the people as their leader, but also aspired to create a culture with similar values.

Chapter 23

Building cultures of integrity

Situation to address

Everyone yearns to work within a culture of integrity, trust and transparency.

However, how can such a culture be most effectively achieved and maintained?

What can you do to achieve and maintain it within your levels of authority?

Suggested mindset and approach

The key is to take the initiative <u>yourself -</u> to insist on being independently evaluated on all key aspects within your authority and your responsibility.

Proactively request that your areas of responsibility should be independently reviewed and checked.

The approach is for all those with authority to go straight to the heart of any matter which could cause themselves or the organization to come under question or scrutiny.

The litmus test is to self-impose independent assurance on any matter which might raise some questioning, as well as those required by regulations, laws or standards.

Results and benefits

By taking the initiative yourself, trust is immediately established.

The person with authority who takes such a proactive approach, will be able to command greater respect, and thus become more impactful.

Excellent governance standards are increasingly at the heart of any organization, especially in respect of individuals with significant authority. By ensuring this self-imposed transparency and evaluation, an individual is able to achieve these high standards and lead rather than follow.

In addition, having a person, or leader, use authority and take the initiative to ensure personal accountability and independent transparency is a powerful catalyst to create a culture of trust and openness across the entire organization.

Such a culture usually increases staff engagement and commitment which also, in turn, reduces staff turnover.

Furthermore, far less time and resources are necessary for matters regarding such assurance – because it is being self-imposed collaboratively and consensually rather than in a confrontational manner.

Ultimately the business can focus time and resources on the matters at hand rather than being distracted by accusations or feelings of potential mistrust.

Impact takeaway

It's not about saying "trust me", rather it's about <u>enabling</u> others to come to their own conclusions.

Making it personal – consider:

1. What is the "trust and transparency" culture like in my workplace?
2. What can I proactively do to help cultivate more of a trusting culture?
3. How can I enable those around me come to their own conclusions?

My role model "shout outs" who…

"Are transparent, and have moral integrity."

Part III
Developing a Better "Me"

Insight from Torah Portion 24 – "Vayikra"

Situation:
Now the Sanctuary's materials have been gathered, the instructions regarding its use and construction are considered.

As this phase starts, God calls out to Moses. The term used for this "calling out" is not only used as the name of the portion, but also as the name of the third (of the five) books of the Torah.

Quote from the Torah:
Leviticus 1:1 "And He called (Vayikra) to Moses…"

Chassidic Insight:
What is so special and important about the word "Vayik**ra**"?

The Torah could have chosen to use another very similar word, "Vayik**ar**", which implies a rather dismissive way of speaking, compared with Vayikra, which implies a loving and very close relationship between the parties.

The only difference between the words in Hebrew is that Vayikra has an additional final letter added to it, namely the Aleph ("א").

We are told that Moses wanted to write the word without this final letter as, in his humility, he did not want to imply that God spoke to him in a close and loving way. God insisted that Moses write it with the "א" so that <u>everyone would know</u> that God recognised special quality attributes within Moses, which engendered His close loving relationship with him.

Moses complied but wrote the letter much smaller than all other letters, so as not to draw attention to the special relationship he had. Thus, he revealed his relationship but with <u>humility</u>. To this day, Torah scrolls have this word written with a small "א", thereby reminding us of Moses's example, namely, to reveal our attributes but with humility.

This is such an important lesson in life. In many circles, this is the first Torah lesson taught to a child - how to acknowledge your unique attributes and strengths.…<u>with humility.</u>

Chapter 24

Should I tell people about my strengths?

Situation to address

Everyone has unique strengths and special attributes.

Is it best to keep quiet about them?

The problem is, if people are unaware of your strengths and special attributes this will reduce the impact and benefit that you could contribute to a given situation by deploying them.

So how should you strike a balance in embracing and making known what your unique skills, attributes and achievements are, whilst not bragging or flaunting them?

Suggested mindset and approach

Firstly, you should <u>self</u>-acknowledge your individual gifts, including unique strengths and ability to positively influence.

Then make others aware of them.

Being too self-effacing, denying your attributes, may well result in a "lost" opportunity to make a positive contribution, one which would be appreciated by others.

The key, however, is that within this sharing of your gifts with others, <u>humility</u> is the name of the game.

This essentially comes about by realizing that your personal strengths and ability to positively influence, are <u>gifts</u> entrusted to you.

A "gift", or giving, mindset, rather than "self-achievement", or arrogant one, enables you to realize how fortunate you are to be given such an attribute. This should help minimise your ego and self-aggrandizement, which only takes away from your performance and impact.

An even deeper and more powerful embodiment of informing others of your strengths and gifts and to enable their contribution with humility is to consider, were someone else to have the same gift, how much better would they deploy it. This highlights the responsibility you have in making other people aware of them – as and when appropriate.

Results and benefits

Letting people know of your strengths and attributes, enables them to be used and to therefore be of benefit to others.

Acting with humility helps others to embrace and utilize them in a much more impactful and authentic way and without making them feel embarrassed that they, themselves, do not have these attributes. After all, it is likely that they have attributes that you don't have! This is because, essentially, one's ego is kept out of the way, enabling you to maximise these gifts to their fullest potential.

The benefits to an individual from this insight is transformational as it enables a grounded, yet determined and ambitious, mindset being applied in utilizing your gifts.

What is even far more impactful is when a leader, manager, mentor or colleague identifies a strength or gift in someone else and enables them to acknowledge, embrace and utilize it with determination and responsibility.

This type of input can transform an individual's life as well as the fortunes of an organization – after all, an organization is only as good as the sum of its parts and, in particular, its people.

Impact takeaway

Know who you are. Be thankful for who you are. Share who you are.

Making it personal – consider:

1. What do people think my unique strengths are?
2. How do I feel about them? Am I grateful for them? Do I view them as gifts?
3. How much more could I utilize my gifts for the benefit of others? Do I see this as my personal duty and responsibility?
4. How could I help others see, acknowledge and utilize the gifts that they have?

My role model "shout outs" who...

➤ "Use unique strengths and gifts with humility."

Insight from Torah Portion 25 – "Tzav"

Situation:
The rules regarding how the Sanctuary should operate continue to be explained. This now includes details regarding the fire on the altar situated in the outside yard.

Quote from the Torah:
Leviticus 6:6 : "A <u>continuous</u> fire shall burn on the (outside) altar; it shall not go out"

Chassidic Insight:
What is the importance of having a <u>continuous</u> fire?.. and why on the outside altar which was visible to all (rather than the more holy golden altar within the inner Sanctuary)?

Everyone has their own personal "Sanctuary", and the altar represents the heart.

Fire represents passion and enthusiasm, and your passion and enthusiasm needs to be visible to all as it brings positivity.

The importance of having a "<u>continuous</u> fire that does not go out", highlights the importance of ensuring you must <u>always endeavour to</u> undertake your obligations, with passion and enthusiasm, regardless of circumstances - even challenging ones.

Thus, you must develop the necessary skills to ensure your personal, external, visible "fires" continuously keep burning with enthusiasm, no matter how your internal moods or situations may vary.

Critically, this outward demonstration of positivity, lights up your own personal internal drive and motivation… <u>hence helping to keep your internal light</u> "fired up".

Chapter 25

Feeling the pressure? - How to behave

Situation to address
How should you behave with others when feeling down, under stress, pressure or any other adverse emotion?

Suggested mindset and approach
Awareness of your demeanour is critical, especially when feeling negative or emotional.

Essentially, despite maybe feeling despondent, pressurized, stressed or some other negative emotion, you should be mindful that, regardless as to what you might be feeling internally, externally you should <u>strive to</u> project an enthusiastic and positive approach.

We are all given challenges, pressures or what we might consider to be 'unfair' stresses and strains. Whilst these are often out of your control, you must work as best as you can to ensure that your emotions are under control.

Always strive to maintain a positive external demeanour. If necessary, a "fake it till you make it" approach should be taken.

Needless to say, mastering personal awareness is key to success.

Results and benefits

Positivity breeds positivity (and vice versa), so having continuous passion and enthusiasm, brings many benefits, including:

- Adopting a positive mindset in and of itself tends to always result in better outcomes, and as a worst case, helps to maintain, a positive atmosphere, regardless of outcome.
- Keeping your enthusiasm "fired and burning" continuously, helps supress and, hopefully, extinguish negativity.
- Positive mindsets are "contagious" and inspire others to also have a "can do" mentality regardless of the situation.
- Essentially, enthusiasm and passion breed positive thought, behaviours and inspiration to others!
- This, in turn, inevitably results in overall better outcomes and more positive and collaborative work environments.

Ultimately, though, by being continuously on "fire" your personal essence, drive and "light" is always on, which, in turn, enables an enhanced personal impact and output.

Impact takeaway

Continuous external positivity, regardless of internal challenges, brings about additional energy and light, not just in others, but also in yourself.

Making it personal – consider:

1. When was the last time I demonstrated less than totally positive passion and enthusiasm in a situation? What was the impact?
2. Compare this, to when positive mindsets have been adopted. How differently did people respond and feel?
3. How is my performance impacted by demonstrating passion and enthusiasm in the workplace? Am I aware of the long-term team and culture benefits?
4. How can I improve my self-awareness to enhance an ongoing demonstration of passion and enthusiasm?

My role model "shout outs" who…

➢ "Demonstrated positivity in the face of adversity and pressure."

Insight from Torah Portion 26 – "Shemini"

Situation:

The Sanctuary has now been completed and is ready to use.

After several attempts the day finally arrives when the Sanctuary has been successfully completed and a fire comes down from heaven and consumes the offering.

Quote from the Torah:

Leviticus 9:1 – "And it was on the eighth day…"

Chassidic Insight:

It was on the *first* day, of the *first* month in the year, that, for the *first* time, an offering was "accepted" by God within the Sanctuary.

The obvious question is, why does the Torah describe this as the "eighth day"?

The answer is because there were seven previous days when offerings were offered, however, without success… and referring to the first day of success as the "eighth day", implies that the success could not have been achieved without the previous "failed" attempts.

Thus, these seven days of "failure" were a critical and fundamental aspect and part of the process in achieving the first ultimate success.

Chapter 26

Dealing with failure

Situation to address

You have a mission/critical goal to achieve.

You try… you fail. Now what?

How should you deal with failed attempts in delivering a mission-critical goal?

Suggested mindset and approach

Accept and acknowledge that achieving success is a journey.

Consider if any achievements have ever succeeded in the first few attempts.

Embrace that without failures you cannot achieve the ultimate success that is being pursued.

As a result, you need a mindset that embraces the failures, and critically learn from them, confident in the knowledge that they are a fundamental part towards ultimate success. Failure is often a necessary prerequisite to learning and improving.

Realize that success is not just about having all the right skills, attributes, resources and attitude, but also about developing the necessary experience in pursuing the ultimate goal.

Failure should not feel like a waste of time and energy, but rather an invaluable lesson, to embrace and move a step closer to ultimate success. As the popular saying goes – a successful salesman is not downhearted by someone who doesn't buy from him, quite the reverse –he considers that he is one doorstep closer to a sale.

Results and benefits

Rather than giving up as a result of failure, the outcome and eventual success is enhanced by embracing and learning from the experience.

In addition, it is an attitude of perseverance and positivity that leads to ultimate success, as it creates an optimistic environment which, in and of itself, helps to bond those associated with the goal to remain committed and inspired.

Ultimately, accepting and embracing failure brings you to true humility, and with this humility, internal strength, insights, resolve and resilience are enhanced, which, in turn, deliver the ultimate success.

Impact takeaway

Failure and "hiccups" are normal, along the path leading to meaningful success. Embrace and acknowledge them.

Making it personal – consider:

1. Have I ever experienced failure? What were the consequences?
2. How do I embrace failure?
3. What can I do to challenge failure in order to learn from it and thereby grow and realize success?

My role model "shout outs" who…

➢ "Levered value and learnings from failure."

Insight from Torah Portion 27 – "Tazria"

Situation:

Now the Sanctuary is operational, the Torah goes on to describe who is "spiritually unclean" and thus unable to enter and partake in it.

We now learn of physically harmless markings, that appear on visible parts of the body, indicating spiritual impurity. These markings, called "Tzara'at", would first need to be confirmed by a Kohen, a priest.

Quote from the Torah:

Leviticus 13: 3; 46 – "The Kohen shall look at the lesion on the skin of his flesh, … if it is a lesion of tzara'at… he shall pronounce him unclean."… "He (who) is unclean, he shall dwell isolated; his dwelling shall be outside the camp".

Chassidic Insight:

What is the connection between a harmless skin discolouration and partaking in the holy Sanctuary? Why does this person need to live apart?

Whilst being harmless, the Tzara'at mark was seen as a sign that a person had incorporated a behavioural fault, which needed to be remedied through introspection in solitude. A correction in behaviour, following introspection, was required to correct the fault, whereby the mark would then disappear. As long as the mark was visible, the person was deemed "unclean" and had to work further on themselves.

The privilege of partaking in the holy Sanctuary was dependent on a person having developed and cleansed their behaviours to be pure.

Nowadays this skin infliction no longer exists. The world would undoubtedly be a better place, if we could only be given these visible signs regarding behavioural faults that need correcting and refining.

Consequently, it reminds us to self-reflect and look for "visible" signs that point towards behaviours that make us "spiritually unclean" and, therefore, require introspection and correction.

Chapter 27
Do I notice my own faults?

Situation to address

What are your faults and to what extent do they really matter?

Do you possess the right attributes and behaviours to match the privileged role and responsibilities that you have been given?

How can faults be correctly identified?

Suggested mindset and approach

Profoundly reflect and consider (at least once a year):

- Do I really know my imperfections?
- Am I as good as I think I am?

More importantly, ask others for their candid thoughts about your values, personality or behaviours and how they might suggest that these could change and improve.

Consider not just what people tell you but also how people have adversely reacted to something you have inadvertently said or done.

Ask yourself if there is a recurring theme within the "adverse" feedback.

Once you feel you have identified the "critical fault/s" that need correcting, confirm your conclusions with those who know you best.

You will then have something to work on which will be covered in more depth in the next chapter!

For now the focus is on:

- Internalising and acknowledging the fault

- Taking the time to be aware of your past behaviours and how the slip ups occurred
- Understanding the negative impacts and consequences which result from the fault.

Results and benefits

The process of self-reflection will not go unnoticed.

Those around you will become aware of your "journey" towards recognizing the faults that need to be addressed. There will be an almost immediate, yet unspoken, respect for your honest self-appraisal.

With this will come a level of support and encouragement, even celebration, as your faults are corrected, and your ways are improved… as covered in the next chapter.

Impact takeaway

If I can recognise imperfections in others, do I understand where *my* key areas of imperfections lie?

Making it personal – consider:

1. How do I view myself? How would I grade my character traits and behaviours?
2. If I can't see any major faults, how can I obtain greater insight to reveal what could benefit from improvement within me?
3. Pick one aspect to improve and consider how I can put aside some "quiet me time" to reflect on this one aspect of improvement.

My role model "shout outs" who…

➢ "Understood their own imperfections and faults."

Insight from Torah Portion 28 – "Metzora"

Situation:

The cleansing process of someone with the spiritual illness, "Tzara'at", is now detailed.

After appropriate self-reflection and fault correction, the marks on the skin disappear. The final part of the cleansing process involves washing one's garments.

Quote from the Torah:

Leviticus 14:8 – "The person being cleansed shall then immerse his garments…"

Chassidic Insight:

Why do the garments and clothing need to be immersed in water and purified?

Garments and clothing are, generally speaking, visible to everyone.

Chassidic teachings discuss how just like the body is clothed in garments, so too is the soul.

The garments of the soul consist of three aspects; (1) actions; (2) speech; and (3) thoughts, which are generally visible, or revealed, to others.

Actions and speech are clearly, visibly apparent to those around. Although more subtle, thought can also be somewhat revealed, by people observing what one is reading, as well as one's visible facial reactions and expressions.

Consequently, the process of "cleaning up one's act", self-correction and purification, <u>ultimately requires</u> a change and improvement in one's spiritual/soul garments, namely in one's actions, speech and thoughts.

Chapter 28

Correcting my faults

Situation to address

How can you correct faults and improve behaviours in an effective and impactful way?

How can you transition from an awareness of a fault to the corrective measures to remove it?

What should a new improved *you* look like?

Suggested mindset and approach

Conscious mindful improvements and changes in your action, speech and thinking is the foundation stone to correcting your faults.

Consider what the new/corrected *you* would look like. What could *you* do, say and think about to demonstrate the necessary corrections?

A critical aspect of this is to ensure that these corrections and improvements are visible to others.

More often than not, when you think about how to improve yourself, it's difficult to know how to start, and proceed to finish, implementing changes.

Even more challenging is to ensure that the changes and improvements are permanent and long lasting. And remember, it is much easier to make small, incremental, changes than to make one big makeover!

A suggested approach is to focus on how to *demonstrate* an improvement, through the garments of the soul, namely actions, speech and revealed thoughts.

The key aspect is to continuously demonstrate these new behaviours whenever relevant.

As this is not a quick fix, a process which you could adopt might include:
- Take the time to be <u>aware</u> of your current behaviours, and not overly worry about inevitable slip ups that will arise from time to time
- Aim for continuous and gradual improvement. A long permanent fix rather than a quick temporary one.
- Notice how the "old you" would have erred, and how the "new you" is improving
- Remind yourself that you can eradicate the fault

Results and benefits

Over time, by persevering with these conscious and repetitive "corrective" behaviours within your actions, speech and thoughts, you will make them not only become second nature, but also become embedded into a "new/improved you".

Essentially, to the outside world it will be clearly apparent that you have "cleaned up your act" in a permanent manner as your faults will no longer be visible.

In the fullness of time your efforts will deliver dividends. Those around you will see how you have changed as they will observe your new 'garments' of actions, speech and thought. They might even mention this to you.

Your credibility will increase. But most important of all, you will become a "better you".

By seeing how you can correct and change yourself into a better person, other people may well feel encouraged to refine and improve their own character traits.

The message and lesson to everyone is one of encouragement to correct and improve behaviours, rather than opt out by saying "this is the way I am… take it or leave it".

Finally, and importantly, this process of refinement is one which takes an individual back to their "pure" essence, stripped of any veneers, and resulting in a true sense of self-worth being experienced by the individual.

Impact takeaway

My faults are corrected through the improved relevant behaviours in my thoughts, speech and actions.

Making it personal – consider:

1. What are the aspects which need changing? Which one requires the most urgent attention?
2. What are the new/additional actions, speech/word and thoughts that I will aim to adopt in various situations, and without which could trigger the adverse behaviours?
3. How can I keep check of how I am able to mitigate and remove this fault/weakness?

My role model "shout outs" who…

➢ "Corrected their own faults."

Insight from Torah Portion 29 – "Acharei"

Situation:

The details and laws regarding Yom Kippur, the holiest day of the Jewish year, are now given... a day of deep spiritual connection and contemplation, devoid of material pleasure.

The opening verse explaining this holiest of days is:

Quote from the Torah:

Leviticus 16:1 – "And the Lord spoke to Moses after the death of Aaron's two sons, when they drew near before the Lord, and they died."

Chassidic Insight:

Why, before describing laws of Yom Kippur, does the Torah refer to an already known event, (namely the death of two of Aaron's, the High Priest's, sons)?

Aaron's sons were holy people, and their sole desire was to dedicate their lives to deep spiritual connection and contemplation, devoid of material pleasure. They effectively became solely focused on the spiritual, to the exclusion of the day to day reality on earth. Because of this, their souls were taken away from the physical world and placed permanently in the spiritual world, resulting in their physical death.

Telling us again of Aaron's sons passing, before explaining the laws of Yom Kippur remind us that:

- *Only limited time (one day a year) should be spent in <u>total</u> spiritual contemplation, to reflect and improve, however;*
- *The whole point of such a day, (which is what Yom Kippur represents) is to "bring down" and make tangible use of the day's reflections, by improving oneself through the inspirations and insights garnered from Yom Kippur.*

Essentially, Yom Kippur is a one-day retreat of pure spiritual connection to your soul and essence, with no material pleasures, with the <u>sole purpose</u> of bringing "inspiration" down to this world, to be <u>actioned</u> in the ensuing year.

Chapter 29

Pause... where is my work and career going?

Situation to address

Should you spend time to contemplate deeply where your career and work is going?

How much time should be spent on this?

What should be the balance between contemplation and action?

Suggested mindset and approach

Carve out a <u>limited</u> period, say a day a year, without any distractions, to enable focused, profound reflections though retreating and reconnecting with your essence.

Ideally a day of solitude, without a phone, and in total quiet. A total pause and break from everyday life. A personal retreat.

A day of minimal indulgence on physical desires, themed with deep contemplation, to objectively assess life - past, present and future.

The key, however, is to restrict this to a day, thereby not falling into the trap of over contemplating work-life.

The structure of the day to consider for personal reflections could include aspects such as:

- Key achievements to date – what have they been?
- Greatest disappointments and regrets
- Towering strengths and unique gifts - what are they?

- "What do I want to be remembered for" … define the ultimate ambitions based upon strengths and gifts.
- What needs to happen over the next five years to realize these?
- If you only had one year to action this, what would be prioritized and actioned?
- Make a committed tangible plan to make it happen.

Importantly, contemplation needs to be based upon core values and meaningful outcomes rather than just financial goals.

The key aspect is to ensure an actionable plan is drafted in which corrections, improvements and new goals and ambitions can be realized and implemented.

Results and benefits

An annual retreat can have a transformational effect and impact in reconsidering work-life, if done properly.

It can result in forming fresh, new, approaches and initiatives as well as re-confirming what is already successful, meaningful and impactful.

Clarity of re-energized purpose and focus are the result.

Limiting this to a relatively concentrated, focused period of time, enables you to take the insights and convert them into action.

This avoids the risks and temptations of getting stuck in always contemplating, and never transforming contemplation into action/implementation.

Incorporating the right setting and environment (such as minimal distractions), enables an objective and clear thinking mindset which, in turn, delivers relevant, insightful and transformational personal insights and goals.

Impact takeaway

Reconnecting and contemplating your core essence and ambitions for one day, breathes a renewed focus and vigour into your goals, which can profoundly impact the rest of the year… and indeed your entire life.

Making it personal – consider:

1. When was the last time I took time out to assess my life, or my team's ambitions? What was the setting, structure and output?
2. Based on the above suggested elements of personal reflections, what do my future plans and aspirations look like?
3. How much has been delivered and realized since?
4. How action orientated was the output, and how quickly were actions implemented?
5. What commitment and actions are needed in order to deliver these life ambitions?

My role model "shout outs" who…

➢ "Balanced realigning life's direction, whilst still moving forward."

Insight from Torah Portion 30 – "Kedoshim"

Situation:

Now that the details regarding the Sanctuary have been addressed, the theme of "working within oneself" continues with how to be holy (ie righteous), and God like. Practical examples are given, including how to harvest a field.

Quote from the Torah:

Leviticus 19:1,2 : "And the Lord spoke to Moses, saying, "Speak to the entire congregation of the children of Israel, and say to them, You shall be <u>holy</u>, for I, the Lord your God, am <u>holy</u>.""

Leviticus 19:9,10: "When you reap the harvest of your land, you shall not fully reap the corner of your field… you shall leave them for the poor."

Chassidic Insight:

Why does the Torah command that a corner of every field should be set aside? What's does this have to do with being holy?

*The critical aspect is that we are **not** told how large the corner of the field should be. It could range from a single stalk to half the field. Being holy and righteous is less about following the "black and white" aspects of life, but more about <u>deciding what is right</u> in the <u>more challenging, tougher decisions in life</u> – i.e. those aspects which are in "the grey zone" and where an individual can exercise discretion.*

In other words, being holy depends on how you apply yourselves to making decisions which are not clear cut. To do this you must consider not what is best for you, but rather to elevate your thought process to consider what God would wish to be done. Consequently, when making decisions in the "grey zone", you should detach from your own ego, and consider what is right from an <u>independent, personally detached, "elevated and holy" perspective</u>.

This is an example of where and how true free choice is applied and expressed in life. This is what it means to behave and live in a holy righteous manner.

Chapter 30

Being a "mensch" with tough decisions

Situation to address

What is the key to making the right choice when faced with tough decisions at work?

In fact, what defines a tough decision?

How can you be a mensch (good and righteous person) when making tough decisions?

Suggested mindset and approach

Tough decisions require having a righteous, independent approach.

Realize that "tough" decisions are essentially defined by a lack of clarity of which action to take, which leaves a bandwidth of choices from which a decision needs to be made.

The point that can often be missed, is confusing a "big" decision with a tough decision.

For example, even though a decision might involve large amounts of money, this doesn't necessarily make it a difficult decision that requires much time contemplating what to do. In other words, despite being a large decision financially, the decision as to what to do is obvious.

By contrast, a tough decision <u>requires judgement</u>, where the correct option is not clear cut. This can cover wide ranging issues such as:

- Whom to fire/hire/promote
- How much to invest

- What to prioritize
- What to buy/sell … etc etc

Once aware of what constitutes a "tough" decision, the next step is to consider how to approach making it.

This is absolutely critical. So often with complex decisions, your own biases or personal views can creep into the final analysis and interfere with the decision itself.

The key approach and mindset to have, however, is that of being personally detached from the decision, and therefore to objectively consider *what is right* from a purely independent and moral perspective.

This process might include asking for a range of independent views, perspectives and opinions as to what to do, to enable a detached and objective approach to making the decision.

Ultimately, tough decisions call for righteous, virtuous, moral and honourable mindsets.

Results and benefits

The benefits of adopting such an approach to true "tough" decisions enables better ultimate decisions.

As well as the benefit of time efficiency which this approach will produce and which will enable you to allocate good, quality time, to arrive at decisions which are truly "tough", the additional benefits include:

- Building confidence with those around you in your "independent, objective and clear" decision making capabilities
- Avoiding the sometimes huge, costs of making wrong or suboptimal decisions, often resulting in U-turns, changes or compromised outcomes
- Realizing the benefits from making the right decision sooner

Ultimately, you gain respect and trust for taking an independent and thoughtful approach in making tough decisions.

Impact takeaway
Detachment of personal bias is the key to approaching really tough decisions.

Making it personal – consider:

1. How have I identified "tough" decisions in the past?
2. How did I approach complex decisions with multiple conclusions?
3. How will I identify tough decisions going forward?
4. How can I detach myself from personal biases or values when faced with tough decisions?
5. What approach could I adopt in the future?

My role model "shout outs" who…

➤ "Had grounded objectivity when making tough decisions."

Insight from Torah Portion 31 – "Emor"

Situation:

The Sanctuary is complete, but the priests (namely the remaining sons of Aaron the high priest), still need to be trained regarding work ethic, traits and culture.

Quote from the Torah:

Leviticus 21:1 – "And the Lord said to Moses: <u>Say</u> to the priests, the sons of Aaron, <u>and say to them</u>…"

Chassidic Insight:

There is a redundancy in the expression "<u>and say to them</u>…", as Moses is already commanded to "say" to the priests.. Why does the Torah include this double expression to "say"?

The commentaries explain that this double expression is to emphasise, that the one giving the instruction has a responsibility to invest the necessary effort, rather than just words, to have an impact and, most importantly, act as a role model, <u>leading by example</u>.

When this happens, the desired behaviours and instructions will shine forth from the instructor's conduct, and thereby illuminate and inspire all those they come in contact with.

In this way, you can better understand how by investing the effort to role model the desired outcome, you are able to influence behaviours and thus cultures.

CHAPTER 31

How can I change the culture?

Situation to address

How can you change or influence the culture of an organization?

Even though you might keep communicating to others what the desired behaviours and culture should be, this does not necessarily have much impact.

Moreover, if a culture is not aligned with the desired goals, then an organization may fail, as the saying goes, "culture eats strategy for breakfast".

Suggested mindset and approach

When developing a desired culture, spend less time on the words and more time on the actions.

Actions and role models are the key to inspiring change and desired cultural values. This enables the benefits to be seen and experienced by others.

The key is to do this sincerely, purposefully, joyfully, positively and with authenticity.

It's that simple!

Results and benefits

The adage that "culture eats strategy for breakfast", becomes a myth when those desiring the changes focus their vast time and effort on being "culture" role models… demonstrating, behaving and living what is wanted.

As a result, positive and contagious behaviours transpire, especially because those who become inspired themselves naturally become role models and inspirational themselves.

Essentially, when you continuously and systematically exude a virtue in your conduct, there is a high probability that your colleagues will adopt it.

Finally, as we endeavour to become role models and teach others, we too, grow. The positive traits which are important to us - and that we therefore seek to impart - become reinforced and strengthened within ourselves through proactively sharing them with others.

Impact takeaway

Role models eat culture for breakfast.

Making it personal – consider:

1. Can I think of examples when a culture or change of program was communicated via words rather than action? How did it go?
2. What has most effectively inspired culture or behaviour change in my workplace?
3. Who are the models that I have most experienced and benefited from? What impact and benefit did they have?
4. What will it take for me to be a role model? How can I make it happen?

My role model "shout outs" who…

➢ "Role modelled desired culture values."

Insight from Torah Portion 32 – "Behar"

Situation:
Whilst still encamped in the Sinai desert, which is where the Ten Commandments were given by God, some of the future laws specific to living in the land of Israel are now communicated.

Quote from the Torah:
Leviticus 25:1 – "And the Lord spoke to Moses on Mount Sinai…"

Chassidic Insight:
Why doesn't the Torah just say Sinai. Why also include the word "on mount", (Behar) as part of the location's identity?

This question is exacerbated, when considering:

- Sinai was primarily known as a desert not a mountain.
- A desert has connotations of nothingness, thus implying humility.
- A mountain, however, has connotations of grandeur and pride.

Given that the name of this portion is "Behar" (on Mount), this implies that there is an important lesson about pride.

The answer is that Mount Sinai, whilst indeed being a mountain, was a relatively small one and thus a "humble" mountain.

It had both qualities, namely (a) the humility of a desert, and (b) the pride and presence of a mountain.

This is to teach us that in life, as well as having humility, one's identity also needs an appropriate amount of self-pride, in order to live a <u>healthy and stable life with a sense of self-esteem.</u>

This aspect of self-esteem, through a combination of pride and humility, was going to be a critical characteristic for the people, especially when the time came to enter the land of Israel.

Chapter 32

Building healthy self-esteem

Situation to address

How should I act in the workplace - modest and meek, or proud?

In fact, is there room for any pride at work? Doesn't that feel like being egotistical?

How can the right balance be achieved in order to establish a healthy level of self-esteem?

Suggested mindset and approach

It is critical to know that having pride is absolutely fundamental to appropriate levels of self-esteem. Without self-esteem there is the risk of you feeling worthless and powerless.

Workplaces can sometimes be tough and therefore you need to have the required strength (as mountains do) to be appropriately resilient.

The right balance is achieved by first acknowledging your strengths, responsibilities and levels of authority.

In doing do, you should certainly be proud of your stature but, critically, coupled <u>with gratitude</u> at having attained that position.

This pride enables confidence and determination to use your strengths, responsibilities and levels of authority but, with humility and gratitude.

The feeling of gratitude comes from reminding yourself that all these attributes are <u>gifts and privileges,</u> bestowed upon you. Moreover, you should, as previously mentioned, contemplate if someone else were to be "blessed" with such attributes, how much better would they use them than you do.

This brings together a blended balance of pride in your "skills and powers", together with the humility and acknowledgment that these are privileges, which must be used responsibly.

You should view yourself as a "small mountain"... namely behave with both pride and humility.

Results and benefits

Essentially, this mindset empowers you to do what is incumbent on an individual and, at the same time, behave with humility knowing that these are "gifts" which someone else might use more effectively than you.

Importantly, this blend of pride and humility enables the use of your positive attributes but without the unhealthy and damaging effect of ego and self-importance.

This results not just in confidence and self-respect in your own worth and abilities; but it also creates a level of respect and appreciation from others.

Without question, this combination of pride and humility will enable your skills and strengths to be used to achieve incredible and inspirational impact.

Impact takeaway

Healthy self-esteem is a blend and balance of pride and humility.

Making it personal – consider:

1. What are my strengths, skills and areas of authority?
2. How do I feel about using them... confident or meek?
3. Do I at times let "power and self-importance" go to my head?
4. What does healthy self-esteem look like to me?
5. What would my "small mountain" behaviours look like? How can I adopt these behaviours in practice?

My role model "shout outs" who...

➢ "Demonstrated healthy self-esteem."

Insight from Torah Portion 33 – "Bechukotai"

Situation:

Commandments in the Torah relate to everyday life. They cover a wide range of instructions, behaviours and choices. Some are obvious, whilst others have no apparent logic or reason. Now the Torah encourages their adoption regardless of understanding (as well as an explanation of some of the blessings which will be bestowed upon those adhering to them).

Quote from the Torah:

Leviticus 26:3 – "If you <u>walk in My statutes</u> and observe My commandments and perform them, …."

Chassidic Insight:

On the surface the rather strange phrase, "<u>walk in My statutes</u>" seems redundant, as it could have simply said, "if you observe My commandments and perform them".

Moreover, the Hebrew word for "<u>statutes</u>" (Bechukotai), relates to the category of commandments which have no logic and are impossible to understand as they have no apparent rationale or purpose.

The lesson behind this is that when it comes to doing the "right thing" (which in this case is God's will), you should not waste time but, instead immediately "<u>walk</u>" in their ways, move forward proactively and <u>do them</u> even if you do not fully understand the rationale for doing so.

The implication is that any delay in walking in their ways will cause you to miss out on part or all of the benefits from doing the right thing.

Furthermore, the statement to encourage the observance of all commandments starts with commandments which have no apparent reason or logic.

This implies that, at the time that one is given good advice and direction it is often the case that one doesn't fully appreciate its benefit and rationale. Despite this lack of understanding, the advice should still be trusted and embraced.

Chapter 33

Taking advice from those you trust

Situation to address

You have received advice from those you *truly trust* and respect regarding your behaviours and life choices.

However, you don't fully understand the rationale.

What should you do?

Suggested mindset and approach

Act now. Follow the instructions given. Understand later.

Simply put, it might just take too long to (ever) fully understand the rationale and benefit of the advice given. As a result, if embracing it is delayed until it is fully understood, you could miss out on the opportunity of acting upon it sooner in your life.

Needless to say, critical to this is ensuring that the advice is coming from a source that you totally trust.

This would normally require that it comes from an independent source with relevant experience and a successful track record, ideally with no vested interest in you taking the advice on board.

There are a wide range of aspects where you can receive trusted advice, embrace it, and act promptly.

As we conclude the third part of the five sections in this book, what advice or suggestions do you feel you could adopt so far?

To summarize:

1. Career focus utilizing and "elevating" the unique skills I have rather than accumulating wealth. Wealth is only the product of successfully deploying my skills (both professional and interpersonal) in the workplace.
2. Putting the right, conscious, effort into having a work-life balance
3. Choosing a career path aligned to who I am
4. Proactively adopting strategies to perform at my best
5. Leaving a lasting impact where I've worked
6. Positively impacting company culture
7. Adopting a personal growth mindset
8. Effectively dealing with conflicts and confrontations
9. Actively applying authentic work interactions
10. Having suitable ambition and vision
11. Always keeping a moral compass (even with huge success)
12. Always being able to survive and thrive in the workplace
13. Not losing my identity at work
14. Approaching huge challenges appropriately and successfully
15. Freeing myself from what's holding me back
16. Dealing with self-doubt
17. Adopting effective delegation
18. Enabling continuous improvement, even if I may be the best
19. Ability to fully share the gifts and unique attributes that I have
20. Being an impactful leader
21. Mindset for true teamwork
22. How to be "emotionally smart" at work
23. Ensuring personal accountability
24. Using my unique strengths with humility
25. Maintaining continuous positivity at work
26. How to approach failure
27. Personal evaluation
28. Being a better me
29. Resetting aspirations and ambitions
30. Getting tough decisions right

31. How to change culture
32. Feeling good about myself in the work-place – self-esteem

Results and benefits

Simply put, the benefit of achieving each suggestion is significant. Putting any one of them on the 'back burner' could result in not realizing your potential and impact.

Prompt action can realize tangible benefits as well as help avoid pitfalls or problems.

The ability to adopt what is right without fully understanding why it is right, by trusting the right people, will rarely go unnoticed.

As a result, it will also inspire others to not miss out or delay, in receiving and utilizing the benefits of trusted advice.

Impact takeaway

Once you become aware of *what* is right,.. Just Do It! ... even before fully understanding *why* it is right.

Making it personal – consider:

1. Have I ever received trusted advice, and delayed adopting it?
2. From the list of ideas already covered, what are my top 5 which have **not** yet been fully adopted?
3. What actions can I now adopt?
4. What methods or strategies can I now adopt to ensure my behaviours and actions are aligned with my right path?

My role model "shout outs" who…

➢ "Quickly adopted good advice."

Part IV
The Leader Within

Insight from Torah Portion 34 – "Bamidbar"

Situation:
Having spent just over a year in the desert since leaving Egypt, Moses is commanded to count the people.

Quote from the Torah:
Numbers 1: 1-2 – "The Lord spoke to Moses …. Take the sum of all the congregation of the children of Israel…"

Chassidic Insight:
Taking a census is normally a job done by relatively low paid administrators. So why was Moses, the leader of the people commanded to do it?

Making the leader responsible for counting each person, reinforces the importance of acknowledging <u>each individual</u>, by the leader.

In addition to this, there is an aspect within Jewish law which states that anything that can be counted individually, can never lose its identity.

So, from this insight we learn how <u>each individual counts</u> and therefore should be appreciated by the leader. Furthermore, even though there are millions of people, no individual can become insignificant and get "lost in the crowd".

Finally, God obviously knew how many people there were so why did he command Moses to count them?

The sages explain, that when you love something, you count it. The counting was, therefore, an expression of God's love for each individual.

Chapter 34

Building a sense of belonging for all

Situation to address

Employee engagement is one of the most critical impacts of effective leadership to delivering an organization's success.

The next two chapters suggest insights to transform engagement.

The first considers the most basic level of engagement, namely, how a leader can ensure that every individual feels a sense of belonging and part of an organization.

How can this be genuinely achieved?

Suggested mindset and approach

Quite simply, a leader needs to <u>acknowledge</u> each and every individual within the organization regardless of their rank and position. This acknowledgement in turn implies that the individual is needed and counts.

Without doubt this is critical for the CEO, but it is also vital for anyone in a leadership role.

Acknowledgement can clearly range from a simple smile to mentioning the individual's name, and even asking about the welfare of something important in the individual's life.

Whilst on the surface this might seem like a "cute" or "nice to have" aspect of an organization, the benefits can be transformational.

Results and benefits

Individuals feel a belonging and genuine engagement to the organization as a result of the acknowledgement and genuine care and concern shown by the leader.

Importantly, this enables the individual to continuously feel engaged and a valued part of the whole.

Furthermore, because of this feeling of "*I am counted and therefore I matter*", individuals will be motivated to demonstrate, through their output and efforts, their self-worth and the unique contribution that they make.

This one simple action can lead to transforming the "staff engagement" metric that so many organizations struggle to impact, despite other efforts.

More importantly the organization benefits not just from a broader sense of belonging but, additionally, the collaboration amongst individuals is enhanced.

Impact takeaway

The fact is, everyone counts,.. so, as a leader "walk the talk" and acknowledge everyone.

Making it personal – consider:

1. How, and how often, do I acknowledge team members or even colleagues?
2. What more could be done to demonstrate my acknowledgement of each one as an individual?
3. How am I going to ensure that acknowledging people will become a key priority, effort and focus (especially if I'm in a position of leadership)?

My role model "shout outs" who…

- "Acknowledges everyone."

Insight from Torah Portion 35 – "Naso"

Situation:

The counting of the people continues, with Moses commanded to count the last remaining tribe.

Quote from the Torah:

Numbers 4: 21-22 – "The Lord spoke to Moses saying: Raise the heads...."

Chassidic Insight:

Why is this rather curious command of "raise the heads" used to continue the counting/census?

This teaches that as well as acknowledging that people count (as per Bamidbar), there is an even more profound aspect, namely, to ensure that each individual <u>understands (i.e. within their heads) as to why they count</u> and are needed.

Thus, not only do the individuals feel their presence is acknowledged, but they all understand specifically what their unique contribution, function and value is.

This new deeper <u>understanding and appreciation,</u> regarding your need and purpose, is equivalent to "raising the head" of the individual to a new level of engagement and belonging.

Chapter 35

Making people feel valued with self-worth

Situation to address

When individuals in an organization understand their self-worth and contribution, this deeper sense of appreciation further enhances staff engagement, resulting in higher motivation and performance.

But how can leaders do this?

Suggested mindset and approach

This next level in staff engagement requires not just an acknowledgment of the individual, but also a concerted focus by the leader, to ensure that each individual <u>understands</u> what, and how important they are, and that they are appreciated by the leader.

Essential to this is for the leader to take the time to understand and appreciate the role and impact of each person. The leader should contemplate how difficult or impossible it would be for the organization to run without each individual performing their specific function.

(A bit like appreciating how every aspect of your body is critical to its optimal function, from the brain to even your toes, … equally, so is every function within an organization).

The leader then needs to articulate and express the impact and importance of <u>each</u> function to each relevant individual, including the consequences to the organization, should the particular function not be fully performed.

Whilst this "specific to every role" approach by a leader, to show individual appreciation, is not an "overnight" task, it is critical for a leader to persevere and ensure it is carried out.

Results and benefits

By receiving an informed acknowledgement from a leader regarding their importance and the potential impact of their role and function, individuals not only feel appreciated and valued in what they do, but they are also more driven to deliver.

This comes about because an individual is aware that their leader understands and appreciates what their <u>unique</u> purpose and impact potential is.

With this comes a feeling of collective appreciation, pride and purpose… which not only impacts individuals but develops a collective culture of "we're in this together" camaraderie, regardless of title and function.

Furthermore, respect and connection to a leader is enhanced, as people appreciate leaders who make other people feel important and valued.

In other words, leaders who understand the importance of each person, and impart that understanding to everyone, are, in essence "lifting everyone's heads" by developing a basis of understanding as to why they count and why they are appreciated.

Impact takeaway

Let me tell you why I value and appreciate you.

Making it personal – consider:

1. Do I understand the importance and potential impact of every role within the scope of my work?
2. What can I do to understand this myself?
3. What can I do to impart and share this "value appreciation" with each person, in respect of the specifics relevant to what they do?

My role model "shout outs" who…

➤ "Develops a sense of self-worth in others."

Insight from Torah Portion 36 – "Beha'alotcha"

Situation:

The command to light the holy seven branched oil candelabra (Menorah) is now given.

Quote from the Torah:

Numbers 8:2 – ""When you cause the lamps to arise…"

Chassidic Insight:

Why describe the process of igniting the lamps as "cause to arise", rather than simply say "light" the lamps?

The use of the word Beha'alotcha, to "_arise_" the lamps, rather than the more usual term "light" the lamps, reflects that a lamp is only fully alight once the flame is able to "arise", and remain lit by itself on the wick.

Pull away a match too quickly, the lamp will not remain ignited on the wick.

However, when you leave the match by the unlit lamp long enough, then the flame on the wick will be ignited, will _arise_ by itself and _remain_ alight even after the match is removed.

The same is applied when imparting wisdom.

Lighting someone up, relates to imparting wisdom to them. From the description of lighting the Menorah, we can learn how to impart wisdom to someone.

Remain close to the recipient until they have grasped the wisdom and can "arise", and use it without the imparter of wisdom being present.

Chapter 36

How to impart impactful wisdom

Situation to address

How should a leader impart wisdom, guidance and direction so that it is received and embedded in the recipients?

Suggested mindset and approach

A leader (or teacher), should "remain" with the recipient of the wisdom, teaching or demonstrating their insight, until satisfied that the idea being shared will continue to be "alight", even after leaving.

Realize that communicating an idea requires the leader to be present until it has been grasped and will likely be adopted.

In practise, the aspect of "remaining" often means revisiting and checking that the new idea or direction has been understood and is being adhered to. Only when the leader is sure that the idea has been adopted and deployed, can he "move away" and stop pushing the idea.

A critical aspect of this approach is for the leader to realize that it is not a shortcoming of the recipient, but rather the leader, if it is not being embraced when the leader is not present.

Results and benefits

Essentially, a leader can only be effective and have impact if the ideas and direction are not only received but also understood and deployed. Without ensuring this critical step, the leader is at risk of failing in this task.

This concept is not limited to leaders, but to any individual who wishes to embed an idea, through others, within an organization.

Furthermore, applying the necessary effort to ensure an idea has been fully received and understood, avoids the risks and potential negative consequences of wrongly making such an assumption.

Impact takeaway

It is the leader's fault if new ideas and direction have not been adopted, not the fault of those being communicated to.

Making it personal – consider:

1. To what extent do I ensure my thoughts and new ideas are fully understood and received by those with whom I share?
2. Have I made the mistake of thinking that an idea communicated, is an idea executed? What were the consequences?
3. Have I ever been frustrated that my ideas shared have not been implemented? Did I put in adequate effort to ensure and satisfy myself that the ideas have been fully understood?
4. What can I do differently in sharing new ideas and wisdom, or insights in the future, to ensure they will become embedded within the organization?

My role model "shout outs" who…

➢ "Skilled at getting new ideas and concepts to be adopted."

Insight from Torah Portion 37 – "Shelach"

Situation:

At the end of the first year after leaving Egypt, there was an opportunity to enter the Land of Israel. However, before doing so, the people wanted to check it out. So, they asked Moses if they could first send some spies to assess the land.

Up until now, Moses was guided by God when communicating to the people. Now, for the first time, God tells Moses to <u>decide for himself</u> whether to send the spies or not.

Quote from the Torah:
Numbers 13:3 – "So Moses sent them …"

Chassidic Insight:

Why did Moses follow the people's wishes to send spies to the land of Israel when it was clear to him that the right thing to do would have been to just go straight into the land, as this was God's repeated command since leaving Egypt?

Moreover, the events that unfurled from the spies' report back, resulted in the people remaining an additional 39 years in the desert!

On the surface, therefore, it seemed that listening to the people was a bad idea, and Moses should have commanded them to go straight into the Land of Israel without first spying it out. However, Moses realized that the people asking to spy out the land first, indicated that they were actually not ready to enter it on Moses' trust.

By listening to, and following the people's wishes, Moses was able to avoid entering the land prematurely, which would have resulted in total failure to inhabit the land and by the people ultimately rejecting it. Eventually, the people entered the land after 40 years in the desert. This allowed enough time to pass to process the years of slavery in Egypt and create a real desire to enter, and the ability to successfully settle in the Land of Israel. By listening to and understanding what the people wanted, Moses as leader, was able to avoid disaster and ensure ultimate success.

Chapter 37

Leadership "101" - Listen first, then follow

Situation to address

Everyone is agreed on a specific goal, however there are a few differing approaches to achieving it.

The "best approach" seems obvious to you, but most others do not agree.

What should you do as leader?

Suggested mindset and approach

After listening, discussing and understanding various positions, if you as leader are still at odds with everyone else, follow <u>their</u> chosen path and approach.

Despite having the authority as a leader to choose your preferred route, and overrule the mass' opinion, you need the humility that the situation falls into one of two scenarios:

1. You are wrong or have missed something in how to achieve the goal.
2. You have failed to prepare and/or transmit the necessary understanding to the team, regarding your approach to achieving the goal, and more time and effort is required.

Both scenarios call for the team's view to be listened to and followed.

First because they are right and, secondly, because one can never achieve anything without the team's "minds and hearts" behind it.

Moreover, without a team's "buy in", any action is almost guaranteed to fail.

So, even if a leader is right, patience and getting his team's 'buy in' might take longer to start the desired initiative but will ultimately achieve the desired outcome quicker.

Only once you feel that team "buy-in" has enough credible "critical mass", is it time to take the desired course of action.

When opposing views are more evenly split, then the approach should be to encourage those aligned with the leaders' views, to assist in the 'buy-in' process and execution of the decision.

Finally, there might be occasions where timing is critical and the "best" approach needs to be taken "now", albeit that the team has a different approach. If this is the case, a leader should be aware of the additional risks, and therefore the additional effort required by him in order to succeed.

Results and benefits

Leadership is ultimately about enabling the "delivery of desired results". The approach of "listen and follow" significantly enhances the ability of achieving this goal, as it is almost impossible to deliver without an aligned team focus.

Moreover, this approach avoids costly mistakes by leaders, which often results from levering authority without 'buy-in'.

These mistakes arise when leaders consider leadership is enforcing the right decisions, rather than ensuring that the way forward is also embraced and accepted.

Ultimately, following this approach of "buy-in", might feel like the longest path to start with but, ultimately, it will be the quickest, shortest, path to deliver the desired goal.

Impact takeaway

True leadership is not simply doing what you feel is right but, rather, first listening and understanding what the people feel is right.

Making it personal – consider:

1. Have I ever been at odds with what everyone wanted to do?
2. How did I approach it? What was the outcome?
3. What have been the challenges in executing a decision where most of the team did not buy-in to it?
4. What steps could be taken going forward to ensure team buy-in?

My role model "shout outs" who…

➢ "Correctly assesses the "mood in the room", before taking action."

Insight from Torah Portion 38 – "Korach"

Situation:
Moses and Aaron's leadership is challenged by Korach, who claimed everyone was equal. It quickly becomes self-evident, after putting them to the test, that Korach's leadership challenge came from an ill-founded place - his own ambition rather than a true sense of purpose. Following the failed rebellion, several miraculous signs were given to prove the validity of the current leadership. One of those signs was a staff, or stick, that blossomed.

Quote from the Torah:
Numbers 17: 21 / 23 – "Moses spoke to the children of Israel, and all their chieftains gave him a staff, and Aaron's staff was amidst their staffs. …. the following day behold, Aaron's staff .. had blossomed! It gave forth blossoms, sprouted buds, and produced ripe almonds."

Chassidic Insight:
Why did only Aaron's staff sprout into an almond tree of all trees, and what's the deeper meaning?

Almond trees have a unique characteristic, namely, they are the first tree to "to lead" the seasonal blossoming and giving of fruit. Just as almond trees have unique characteristics, so do individuals, and so Aaron was chosen to be the High Priest because he had the necessary attributes. Whilst this characteristic can be viewed as unique and desirable, one would never want to be in a place which only had almond trees, (or just High Priests), nor to have all trees giving fruit at exactly the same time. In fact, every type of tree has a unique place, bringing its own distinctive attribute to the world.

Hence, rather than wanting to have the attributes or positions of others, one should accept, be grateful for and focus on one's own unique attributes and make those flourish and blossom. Furthermore, successful leadership does not result from envious desires… but rather from a "natural order" of selecting individuals who have the right skills and humble ambition to utilize them for everyone's benefit.

Chapter 38

Get to the top of your ladder, not the ladder

Situation to address

How should you manage your ambitions and desires as well as managing the ambitions and desires of others?

What does "getting to the top" mean for you?

Suggested mindset and approach

At the heart of any ambition should be a focus on "being yourself". In other words, "be who you are meant to be", rather than strive to be someone else.

Understand what your relative strengths are and focus on maximizing the impact and benefit from these. From this basis you should certainly set ambitious goals based on these strengths.

Your ambitions should not be based on simply desiring power, authority or rewards enjoyed by others… but rather on the positive impact created, as a result of using your key, unique, skills and strengths.

An equally important aspect is understanding where colleagues' ambitions are coming from. If it is from a place which matches their strengths, you can play an active role in encouraging them.

However, if ambition is coming from an envious or "ego" driven desire, not aligned with your strengths, such ambitions should be discouraged.

Moreover, as well as not being realized, the danger of pursuing such ambitions is that this can cause divisions, splitting up teams, in attempts to recruit "supporters".

These situations should therefore be discouraged. Without question, being part of such a "rebellion", should be avoided at all costs as they rarely, if ever, turn into sustainable and stable successes.

In such rebellious situations, wisely put the "rebels" to the test to flush them out.

Moreover, if your leadership is being threatened, objectively consider if they are justified or not. As hard as it might be, if it is, humble yourself to them – be magnanimous.

Results and benefits

By focusing on their unique strengths people with "pure" ambition will attain the optimum result and position for both themselves and the organization – there will be an alignment.

Likewise, being aware of what might be motivating the ambition of others will enable you to either support them or, alternatively, avoid/counter them. Ultimately, constructive ambition will lead to realizing growth within an organization.

Conversely, identifying misplaced ambitions will avoid personal and organizational damage and unnecessary distraction.

With this approach the "true" leaders are duly, justly and naturally appointed across all areas of an organization, aligning individuals' strengths with desired goals. This will enable an organization to be optimally led and thereby flourish.

In addition to this, "managing ambition" appropriately will build trust and cohesiveness which, in and of itself, is invaluable.

Ultimately, in the hardest of all situations, when your leadership itself is being justly challenged, embracing and even encouraging and facilitating the challenge will enable you to not only retain your self respect, but garner respect from others too.

Furthermore, adopting this approach for misplaced challenges by others will enable them to be quickly flushed out.

Impact takeaway

Focusing ambition for everyone on simply being "the best you"… enables each individual to achieve their best and, thereby, enables the organization to perform at its best.

Making it personal – consider:

1. Have there been any misplaced ambitions, either by myself or others, in the organizations in which I've worked? If so what were they?
2. Have I experienced natural leadership?
3. What were the consequences of both these situations? How did the culture and atmosphere feel?
4. How do my, or others, natural strengths align with the ambitions?
5. How could I commit to guiding and encouraging others on what their ambition should be and how they might achieve them?

My role model "shout outs" who…

➢ "Aligning personal ambition within natural strengths."

Insight from Torah Portion 39 – "Chukat"

Situation:

Now in the fortieth and last year, in the desert, the command how to purify people is given. It involves taking a mixture of ashes and water and sprinkling it on the 'impure'.

As well as this process being totally illogical and irrational, there's a catch; namely, that at the outset the person who does the purifying needs to be pure himself, but as a result of purifying others, he becomes impure until nightfall.

Quote from the Torah:

*Numbers 19:2 – "This is **the** statute (command) of the Torah…"*

Chassidic Insight:

*Why is this command to purify someone, referred to as "**the**" command of the Torah?*

Furthermore, how is it that this apparently most important of all commandments is the most complex and impossible to comprehend or fathom (which even King Solomon, the wisest of all, could not understand).

The essential lesson is that one can never fathom how much benefit comes from helping someone in need, even if it puts you out, as in the case of the purifier, who needs to be pure before the process, but who, as a result of the process, becomes impure till nightfall.

*This is "**the**" central, most important message of the whole Torah. Namely, to help your fellow… even if it puts you out or causes you inconvenience.*

Chapter 39

The ultimate act of responsible behaviour

Situation to address

A colleague needs my help, but it is really inconvenient.

What should I do?

Suggested mindset and approach

Just help them.

Who are you to say that helping someone in need is not more important than what you feel you have to do?

Realize that there is no way you can fully fathom the benefit and positive impact from helping a colleague in need.

Consider if whatever inconvenience you might have to go through to help someone, has greater negative impact, than the positive impact achieved by helping someone.

In addition to this, contemplate how, most aspects of any job, at any time, can either wait, or be done by someone else, whilst you first help someone out.

Finally consider… "If I needed the help, would I want someone to inconvenience themselves for me?"

Results and benefits

The impact of selfless camaraderie goes a long way in establishing and inspiring an invaluable work environment and culture.

The net benefit to the person, as well as the positive impact on the organization, invariably far outweighs the "cost" and inconvenience to the person giving the help.

In many ways this type of help can have the greatest positive impact relative to any other action taken by an individual.

Impact takeaway

My greatest impact at work might well be to help a colleague rather than to do my job.

Making it personal – consider:

1. What do I feel when I am asked to help and it's an inconvenience?
2. Have I ever given the excuse "I'm too busy"? Why was this?
3. Did I fully understand the benefits of helping a colleague, compared to my inconvenience?
4. Going forward, what changes to my thought process will result in me helping out?

My role model "shout outs" who…

- "Selflessly helped others."

Insight from Torah Portion 40 – "Balak"

Situation:

As the Jewish people approached the land of Israel, despite offering to pay for peaceful passage through the land of the Amorites, they encountered opposition and battle.

The Amorites were quickly and easily conquered.

Balak was the king of the land of Moab. He had secret alliances with the Amorites who bordered his land, hoping that they would be his first and primary line of defence.

Quote from the Torah:

*Numbers 22: 2-3 – "Balak …. saw all that Israel had done to the Amorites, .. and **Moab was afraid** of Israel.."*

Chassidic Insight:

How did the people of Moab become afraid, when it was only Balak, their leader and king, who knew that his secret defences had been destroyed?

From this we learn that Balak had transmitted his fear to the people, who were subsequently conquered.

This is juxtaposed to Moses's approach who, whilst being fearful of the battles from the Amorites, instilled confidence into the Jewish people which resulted in victory.

From this we learn the importance for a leader to contain fear and, instead, imbue confidence.

Chapter 40

Instilling confidence versus fear

Situation to address

The business is in a tough situation.

As leader, you appreciate the severity of the situation more than most. You're afraid of the potential consequences.

When you feel fearful and 'up against it' as a leader, how should you deal with it?

Suggested mindset and approach

Keep the fears to yourself. Remain focused on the task at hand.

Objectively assess the source of your fears as, often, fears cloud judgement as to how to best deal with a situation, as well as not seeing things for what they are.

Ensure that any approach in dealing with the challenge at hand does not come from a place of fear, but rather from a place of clarity.

Critically, be extra mindful and conscious as to how you are coming across to your team and your colleagues. Is your speech faster and more tense than usual? Are you more impatient or curt?

Ultimately, leaders need to know that they have a duty and responsibility to contain and manage their fears, in order to avoid unnecessary negativity.

Rather, despite the challenges, the leader should inspire objective confidence.

Results and benefits

Challenges are addressed with clarity, objectivity and focused relevant efforts… and thus have a much better chance of being successfully resolved.

Avoiding "group fear", naturally helps to mitigate the risks posed by the challenge at hand, and heightens the chances of success, by focusing on the tasks required to successfully address each challenge.

Moreover, teams are encouraged by the calm decisive manner with which leaders approach tough situations, which, in turn, inspires confidence and a determined approach to deal with the situation at hand.

Impact takeaway

Revealed emotions are contagious. As leader, keep fear to yourself …. Better to be hard on the issue at hand with clarity and determination.

Making it personal – consider:

1. Have I ever felt afraid? Did anyone else sense my fears?
2. What were the consequences of others sensing my fears?
3. How could I manage any fears going forward? (Would having a trusted confidant or mentor be useful to talk through it?)
4. How can I keep a focused, positive, confidence enhancing approach with my teams, whilst facing challenging situations?

My role model "shout outs" who…

- "Transmitted confidence, rather than fear to others."

Insight from Torah Portion 41 – "Pinchas"

Situation:

During an act of open immorality and disrespect to God by two powerful and influential people, a plague broke out amongst the people as nothing was being done to stop the immoral acts.

Pinchas, an "ordinary and peaceful person" with no position of leadership, realized something had to be done and that no one was acting.

He realized that the instigators had to be stopped, and so with Moses' knowledge, <u>despite having no obligation to act</u>, and whilst selflessly risking his own life and going against his nature, Pinchas acted to stop them. As a result, the plague ceased.

Quote from the Torah:

Numbers 25:10-13 – "The Lord spoke to Moses saying, "Pinchas … has turned My anger away from the children of Israel by his zealously avenging Me **amongst them**… I hereby give him My covenant of peace… for him and for his descendants after him [as] an eternal covenant of priesthood".

Chassidic Insight:

The words "amongst them" seem totally superfluous, as on the surface were they to be deleted the key message remain unchanged. In addition, a fundamental aspect of Torah is that no letter, let alone word, is unnecessary. So why were these words included?

The words "amongst them" teach us that Pinchas's selfless bravery and uncharacteristic action, was conducted in such a manner as to maintain <u>unity</u> within the community. As a result of this Pinchas and his descendants received an eternal reward from God.

Despite being a junior member of the people, he took the lead and initiative to realize a significant positive impact, by behaving without self-interest, aggrandisement or desire to draw attention to himself, as he resolved a critical, emergency.

Chapter 41

Taking the lead as a junior

Situation to address

You are a junior member of your team, there's a leadership vacuum.

Should you ever step in and take the lead? If so, when and how?

Suggested mindset and approach

Clarity, objectivity and humility are required in taking a leadership action which one normally does not have the authority or responsibility to take.

Examples of business situations that might require urgent, "in the moment" action, could range from making on the spot offers to close a deal, to taking a stand to protect the reputation of an organization.

This requires appropriate, "in the moment" assessment as to whether there is a real <u>and</u> urgent need for action to protect and enhance the organization, as well as absolute clarity, as to what action is required.

Furthermore, it is vital to assess whether others, especially superiors, are considering taking some action.

Once this is assessed, it is critical to ensure that your actions are carried out in a way that does not fragment the team, nor draw undue attention or importance to yourself.

Despite the significant impact the action will likely have, it should be performed with humility.

Moreover, such actions, by definition, carry great potential personal risk, nonetheless, despite this risk, they need to be conducted with confidence and determination.

Ultimately, leadership should create a culture where permission is given for such "subordinate" actions, as well as appropriate appreciation and award offered when correctly applied.

Results and benefits

Ultimately, despite being initiated by a relatively junior member of the organization, huge benefits can flow, which even the greatest and most powerful leaders can sometimes fail to achieve.

Leaders who create cultures that allow junior members to suggest and act, can transform the fortunes of a business.

From this, all members of an organization feel, that under certain conditions, they too have responsibility to lead and deliver positive impact.

A team of people with this attitude will enable an organization to reap untold value as well as, of course, the individuals involved.

Also, this type of culture takes pressure off the leaders to always have to come up with solutions and, rather, give the less senior staffers permission and encouragement to tap into the huge reservoir of skills, wisdom and insights, that exist across the business.

Finally, in healthy "value for value" cultures, the individuals who take wise, brave and impactful actions, will, and indeed should, be rewarded very handsomely, both within the organization structure and with financial compensation. This recognition will, in turn, encourage others to initiate similar behaviours and actions.

Impact takeaway

Encourage self-belief and courage from everyone …. the greatest impact and benefits can come from the most junior members.

Making it personal – consider:

1. Ever felt pressure as a leader to always have to come up with the answers to an urgent and important issue?

2. As a leader, do I create a culture to give permission even to the most junior members to take great personal risk, and suggest ways forward, in a "safe" non-judgemental environment?
3. As a junior, have I or my colleagues ever "seen the light" regarding what to do? Did I speak up? If not why not?
4. What can I do going forward, be it as a leader or junior, to ensure the right urgent actions are taken when needed?
5. How will I be able to act with humility, focusing on what is best for the organization, without any concern for self-aggrandizement, whilst at the same time ensuring unity is maintained?
6. As a leader, am I willing to go beyond the norms in rewarding 'over and above' behaviours from juniors?

My role model "shout outs" who…

➢ "Empowered junior members to take initiative."

Insight from Torah Portion 42 – "Matot"

Situation:
Forty years of Divine miraculous revelation in the desert were about to come to an end as the people were going to imminently enter the land of Israel and the more normal "laws of nature" would prevail. Moses now speaks to the heads, the leaders of the tribes, but this time rather than using the word "Shevatim" for tribes he uses the word "Matot" instead.

Quote from the Torah:
Numbers 30:2 – "Moses spoke to the heads of the tribes (Matot)….."

Chassidic Insight:
Why is the term "Matot" now used to refer to the tribes? The words "Shevatim" and "Matot" both mean "tribes". They also both have another meaning namely (wooden) "staffs", as each leader had their own staff. There is, however, a difference in the nature of a staff depending on whether it falls in the category of Shevatim or Matot.

Shevatim relate to pliable, flexible boughs, freshly cut from a tree, with the sap, freshness and leaves of the tree still present. As a result, there is no question that the staff was connected to a tree, and it was its source of life. Matot, on the other hand, connotes dried out rigid sticks or rods, cut from a tree some time ago, with any external characteristics from the tree having long faded and withered away. The original connection to a tree is far less obvious, and so a deeper contemplation and reflection is required to be aware of the stick's origin.

By using the word "Matot" here, Moses was giving the leaders a critical message, namely, that a different, firmer less flexible leadership style would be needed going forward, because the miraculous revelations and reminders of their true mission were about to stop. Their leadership would now need to adapt this <u>less flexible style</u> and they would also need to establish initiatives to develop a <u>deep rooted and ongoing connection</u> to the mission, in order to ensure a timeless adherence to it. Thus, more effort on the leaders' behalf would be required, to enable the people to <u>remain connected</u> and conscious of their combined mission, goals and purpose.

Chapter 42

How leaders can persevere with the mission

Situation to address

Maintaining the long-term core values, strategic direction and priorities of an organization is critical to its ongoing growth and sustainability.

How can leaders persevere and stay on course over the passage of time?

After some time has passed, their inspiration and clarity and that of their teams may reduce or even wither away.

What is a leader to do? How can clarity and focus on values be kept in the front of the mind, especially during key decision making?

Suggested mindset and approach

Firstly, one needs to realize that, over time, there will be an inevitable "fading" of an organization's once clear founding values, purpose and principles.

Acknowledge that the impact of key missions and goals coming from a corporate conference, training course, or meeting with the CEO, founder or major stakeholders, reduces over time.

Given this, simple techniques need to be developed to keep them firmly embedded within the organization.

Adopting these techniques requires developing a range of structured initiatives to remind and re-inspire everyone towards the mission, goals, purpose and strategy.

By way of example these can include:
- Write and publicize reminders of key goals across banners/websites

- Speak about the principles on a regular basis with teams and colleagues, ensuring they are strictly aligned with the original values and vision
- Reinforce them within the organization's recognition/rewards schemes.
- Proactively acknowledge behaviours which are aligned with the founding vision and messages.
- Develop systems, procedures, governance and controls regarding major decisions, to ensure that the organization's core values and principles are at the core of decision making

Results and benefits

Having a leadership which is continuously putting in effort and energy consummate to what is aligned with the organization's goals and strategic priorities, will keep focus and thus enhance the likelihood of success.

Furthermore, leadership which is continuously operating in accordance with what is most relevant to the organization's expressed aims, will enable an aligned and collaborative approach to achieving them.

This approach will give the overall organization a refreshed focus on what is needed, with limited confusion and inefficiency.

Ultimately, the organization will be better placed to "keep on track" and avoid the risk of leaders not having 'front of mind' what is most important to the organization. It will help keep it from losing its way.

Impact takeaway

Leaders need to find ways to continuously stay aligned and connected to the mission, its purpose and values.

Making it personal – consider:

1. Has my connection and conscious awareness of my organization's missions, goals and purpose changed over time? If so how would I describe the change?
2. What could be done to ensure they are always fresh and top of my mind?

3. Do I, my colleagues and leaders, appreciate the importance of this strategy / discipline?
4. How much effort is required to achieve this?
5. Am I up to the challenge to ensure this can be achieved? What steps are required from me?

My role model "shout outs" who…

➢ "Persevered in steering the course."

Insight from Torah Portion 43 – "Massei"

Situation:

Having completed the last leg of the journey in the desert before the ultimate goal of entering Israel, Moses, as the leader of the people, reflects on the various times when, for whatever reason, the journey halted and paused and thus needed to re-start:

Quote from the Torah:

Numbers 33:1 – 2: "These are the journeys of the children of Israel who left from the land of Egypt …. under the charge of Moses … Moses recorded their starting points … and these were their journeys with their starting points"

Chassidic Insight:

With the current phase of the journey in the desert coming to an end, Moses recounted the various pauses and "re-starts" to the journey.

On the surface any pause in a journey would appear to slow down progress, or even potentially set it back. Why, then, did Moses go to the trouble of recording them?

The answer is that any pause, even a setback or disruption to your life journey, highlights a limitation that is holding you back.

By reviewing and learning what happened during a pause, you can remove a limitation which may be holding you back, uncover a new potential within and thus enable a continuation, bringing greater progress and growth. As a result, the pauses, interruptions and setbacks are a critical and transformational part of your continuing development.

Consequently, as leader, Moses took the time to reflect and appreciate how each pause in their journey had forged a particular growth and development opportunity enabling the climactic stage of entering Israel.

In addition to this was his message that, any future setbacks or pauses should be embraced by the people to enable a stronger "re-start" and opportunity for further growth going forward.

Chapter 43

Leadership when progress stalls

Situation to address

At times, progress in achieving a stated goal stalls. Moreover, setbacks can occur from time to time.

How should leaders deal with such pauses, interruptions and setbacks when in pursuit of the organization's vision?

Suggested mindset and approach

It is critical for leaders to know and appreciate that all pauses, interruptions and setbacks are a part of the overall journey to achieve ultimate success.

Essentially, they are opportunities for learning and growth.

As a result, it is critical <u>not</u> to ignore them, or view them as "annoying" bumps in the road but, rather, as essential episodes for a leader to draw attention to, in order to learn and propel the team to ultimate success.

To enable this to happen, a leader should pause and emphasise to the team what exactly "went wrong", so that everyone has the opportunity to understand the pause or setback, to learn from it and establish strategies to progress from the experience.

Results and benefits

Any pause or setback, no matter how large or small, becomes an opportunity for growth.

With this mind-set, when leaders approach these situations with a positive attitude, negativity that could otherwise spread across the team is avoided and mitigated.

With skilful leadership, everyone feels inspired to create an even stronger, wiser and more capable team.

Learning from setbacks also builds positivity, confidence and resilience which, in turn, contributes to developing a more capable team, delivering higher performance, and with an ability to achieve ever more demanding goals and ambitions.

Thus, each stop, even those that appear as setbacks and wrong turns, are points of learning, and provide a new perception, awareness and sensitivity.

In summary, any setback can be transformed into the ultimate best path to eventual success.

Impact takeaway

True leaders transform setbacks into growth… capitalizing on the opportunities and teachings which they offer.

Making it personal – consider:

1. Has my team ever had a set back? If so, how did I approach it?
2. How could I have spent the time and effort to collectively capitalize on the experience to grow, learn and become more successful going forward?
3. How can future setbacks be levered to realize the opportunity these experiences/events have to offer?

My role model "shout outs" who…

➢ "Revealed the benefits from setbacks."

Part V
Delivering the Strategy and Mission

Insight from Torah Portion 44 – "Devarim"

Situation:

Moses is in his last 37 days before his passing.

The first four books of the Torah are the words spoken by God. The final, fifth book, of the Torah is different in that it consists of the 'farewell speech' that Moses spoke to the children of Israel during these last 37 days.

Quote from the Torah:

Deuteronomy 1:1 – "These are the words which Moses spoke to all Israel…"

Chassidic Insight:

For the first time the words included in the Torah are coming from Moses as the "author", rather than God. Moses is recounting what the people of Israel already know but, this time, in his own words.

Why does the Torah dedicate an entire book to something that comes from Moses rather than God, especially as what Moses is saying has already been covered in the first four books of the Torah?

By the Torah including Moses' own words, rather than instructions from God, we learn the critical and fundamental importance of internalising and personalizing key messages and lessons in life. This process, in turn, enables the messages and lessons to be internalised by each individual and then embraced and incorporated into our everyday lives.

This key lesson was given to the people of Israel to encourage and inspire them to take the time and effort to internalise the infinite messages within the Torah and make them their own.

Moses, was so "at one" with God, due to his humility and self-nullification, (see Chapter 54), that his words were included within the Torah as the fifth book, as if they came directly from God.

This reminds us to be authentic, true, humble and honest, embracing, internalising and then sharing critical messages.

Chapter 44

Ensuring everyone embraces the mission

Situation to address

All too often a company's CEO struggles when the mission statement, key goals or priorities are not fully understood and embraced by everyone.

As a result, optimum behaviours, attitudes and focus are lacking.

How can this be fixed so that there is a universal, clear understanding, so that everyone can embrace the organization's mission, purpose and values?

Suggested mindset and approach

<u>Personalized</u> understanding is the key behaviour and approach to be established.

If you want to assess how a key message has been received, understood and embraced by others, ask them to express their understanding <u>in their own words</u>.

If you want to make sure your understanding is aligned with the organization, then articulate your interpretation to someone in "authority", perhaps from whom you received the original message.

This way the level of understanding and alignment of the message can be confirmed.

All too often, important messages and guiding principles of organizations suffer from "top down" mantras, with little attempt to ensure that they have been properly understood.

Frequently, at best, only a small minority of an organization will really "get it" - the mission statement or strategic goal.

So, in summary, the most impactful way to ensure understanding is to encourage people to explain, in their own words, what they understand the message to be.

Results and benefits

This approach identifies any gaps in understanding or knowledge, as well as enabling a deeper consciousness and understanding of what the organization's ambitions and goals are, rather than a periphery or superficial view.

The result of this additional clarity and understanding is a more determined, collaborative and confident execution and realization of the organisation's mission, strategy and goals.

Furthermore, achieving them is quicker with longer lasting, more sustainable benefits and impact.

Critically, because of the deeper "engraving" and understanding by people articulating key messages in their own words, they will more likely be adopted and have a far longer impact.

Finally, staff and team engagement will also tend to be more meaningful and constructive due to the greater commonality in understanding as well as building a culture of greater confidence by delivering what was envisioned due to the collective clarity.

Impact takeaway

Personalized expression of key missions, values and goals, enables a deeper collective understanding, which in turn facilitates their realization.

Making it personal – consider:

1. Ever had a company mission or goal that never really transitioned into the collective, joined-up behaviour shift needed to deliver it?
2. What did it feel like? Why did only some people get it and get enthused whereas others perhaps even ignored it?

3. How much of the communication was "top down" and failed to ensure that each individual articulated what it meant to them, and checked that their understanding was aligned?
4. How could I consider the best way to communicate future key missions and goals?
5. How could I ensure a process of individual personalization in the future?

My role model "shout outs" who...

➢ "Ensure that those who need to, articulate and demonstrate their understanding of the strategy and key goals."

Insight from Torah Portion 45 – "Va'etchanan"

Situation:

One of the key events that Moses repeats in his last days is the giving of the Ten Commandments. In the first commandment, God introduces Himself to the people.

Quote from the Torah:

Deuteronomy 5:6 – "I am the Lord your God, Who took you out of the land of Egypt, out of the house of slavery."

Chassidic Insight:

Why did God introduce Himself as ".. Who took you out of Egypt"?

God could have described Himself in a much more impressive way, namely as the creator of the universe.

God was not looking to impress the people but rather _connect_ with them.

Hence, he chose to introduce Himself with a "lesser" attribute, namely the One who took them out of Egypt and slavery, as this was an aspect which the people directly experienced.

Thus, because of this, the people could directly _relate_ to God, when He first spoke to them. God related to the people on _their_ level and from _their_ perspective and set of experiences.

As a result, a much closer eternal _bond and connection_ between the people and God was established.

Chapter 45

Relatability... building connected cultures

Situation to address

Organizational cultures are often disjointed, with people across the board feeling disconnected with one another.

Success in delivering strategies and critical missions is dependent on having a cohesive and coordinated culture across an organization. However, this challenge is all too often a stumbling block to ultimate success.

How can organizations overcome these challenges and build strong <u>connections</u> across people in different jobs, positions of seniority or departments?

Suggested mindset and approach

Consciously connect on an aspect in which other parties can directly <u>relate</u> to. Perhaps something which is important to them, or through an impactful experience they have been involved in.

Rather than demonstrate your most impressive attribute, choose attributes that the people with whom you are trying to connect, can directly relate to, from the interactions that they have already had with you.

This requires thought and reflection.

Importantly, building empathy, respect and connection through relatability can be applied to all aspects of an organization, from different levels of hierarchy and across departments and functions.

A CEO, for example, whilst being responsible for a multi-billion-dollar budget, could build a stronger connection with factory floor workers, by directly relating with them and discussing, say, the benefits of acquiring a new piece of machinery which they have requested.

Likewise, when people from totally different areas in the business want to connect, it is best to relate how they can benefit from, and connect, with one another.

Essentially, contemplating how every person, function or department <u>inter-relate</u> with the organization's mission and "value chain", can form a basis for connection and mutual appreciation.

Results and benefits

Building mutual understanding of how different people and teams relate to one another, results in a truer, more authentic and empathetic bond between them.

This, in turn, will result in stronger, longer lasting connections, and a more cohesive culture.

Importantly, by building mutual understanding, people will naturally wish to respect and perform for the parties that have made the effort to explain the aspects of connection and relatability.

As a result, sustainable empathy and collaboration is established which, in turn, strengthens staff engagement and belonging, as well as producing a superior output and impact.

Impact takeaway

Establishing relatability across an organization fuels greater success and collaboration.

Making it personal – consider:

1. Do I explain your role and function in a way that people can relate to from their perspective and set of experiences?
2. What would be the benefits if I understood what everyone did in so far as it impacts me?
3. What steps can, and will, I take to ensure others understand what I do?

4. How can I encourage a mind-set of establishing "relatability" across my organization?

My role model "shout outs" who…

➤ "Relates to people on their terms."

Insight from Torah Portion 46 – "Eikev"

Situation:

Moses now explains the blessings that will flow from adhering to God's commandments.

Quote from the Torah:

Deuteronomy 7:12-13 – "And it will be, ***if*** (Eikev) you will heed these ordinances …. He (God), will <u>love you and bless</u> you…"

Chassidic Insight:

There are a number of Hebrew words for "if". Why is the less common word "Eikev" used in the Torah? (Which also is the name of this portion).

"Eikev" also means "heel" (i.e. of one's foot).

So, why should "love and blessings" be associated with such an inelegant part of the body?

The answer becomes more apparent when we consider that a heel is arguably the most "<u>obedient</u>" part of the body.

You are more likely to use your heel to test whether water is too hot or cold, as opposed to any other part of your body.

In many ways, because it is the hardiest, least sensitive, part of the body, it is also most readily compliant and obedient to your wishes.

From this we learn that by us becoming completely obedient and readily compliant to do God's Will without ego, He, in turn, goes beyond the natural order to <u>love</u> us and bestow abundant <u>blessings upon us</u>.

Chapter 46

The Power of the Obedient Follower

Situation to address

Business success is often described in terms of leadership, but rarely in terms of following instructions.

Ultimate success however is totally dependent on those being led to implement the instructions. After all, nothing ultimately happens without implementation and adherence to directions.

It is therefore important to understand the behaviours of those receiving the instructions.

So how should following instructions be approached in order to deliver the greatest impact?

Suggested mindset and approach

When following agreed instructions from your leader, you should be fully immersed in performing whatever tasks are required, to successfully discharge those tasks.

You should not incorporate any other agenda, but rather, focus on doing exactly what has been requested, whole heartedly and with no ego or thoughts of oneself (very similar to that of a heel in one's foot being totally obedient to the commands coming from the head).

In conjunction with this, a leader giving instructions needs to be acutely aware that a successful outcome is totally dependent upon his instructions being carefully followed.

Thus, as CEO/leader, there needs to be mindful appreciation of those executing their instructions, for whilst it is important to make the right decisions and give the right direction, they are meaningless without execution.

Appreciation and rewards ("love and blessings") need to be given by the leader, acknowledging that it is the <u>quality of following</u> instructions that has generated a task's successful outcome.

Results and benefits

Collective obedience in following instructions with egoless conformity, enables optimum impact in a task's successful execution.

Furthermore, appreciation by the CEO/leader will enhance the required "egoless obedience" by those required to implement the task.

This, in turn, manifests in "blessings", being the recognition and appreciation of following the instructions and successfully delivering the tasks.

In addition, the connection between the "instruction giver" and "implementer" is significantly enhanced and strengthened, resulting in a deeper "love", respect and connection between the two.

In summary, just as your head is carried by the heels, the wishes of the "head" of an organization can only be carried out by those performing them with total obedience.

Impact takeaway

The power of a follower… it's all about implementation at the end of the day… There is nothing like the impact and value realized from an intelligent and obedient follower.

Making it personal – consider:

1. Do I realize and appreciate the importance and value derived from "expert" obedient followers?
2. How much effort and importance is put into ensuring there is alignment in critical instructions?

3. How can the understanding and appreciation of "obedient" execution be improved... rather than the usual "blanket" statements regarding how important execution is in general?
4. How can more be expressed about the value of "followers", rather than the libraries already filled with the value of great leaders?

My role model "shout outs" who...

➢ "Acknowledge and appreciate those who execute required actions and follow instructions."

Insight from Torah Portion 47 - "Re'eh"

Situation:
As his life on earth comes to an end, Moses continues to impart advice and guidance from God.

Quote from the Torah:
Deuteronomy 11:26 – "<u>See</u>, I give before you today a blessing and a curse...."

Chassidic Insight:
The word "see" (Re'eh) seems redundant, as the line could have simply said "I give before you today a blessing and a curse...".
So why include the word "see"?
There are a number of key "life" insights and lessons from this, including:

- <u>Seeing</u> a situation for what it is, is critical to making the right choice, as it enables clarity and objectivity without being hindered by personal biases.
- <u>Seeing</u> blessings in life is instrumental to appreciating so many things which are all too often taken for granted.
- <u>Seeing</u> curses (whether we understand why we experience them or not) is also important, <u>as God only gives "good"</u>. Thus, any perceived curses that occur should be approached with a mind-set of <u>revealing</u> the good that is hidden within them.

Ultimately, the power of objectively seeing a situation for what it is, is critical in determining the correct way to deal with it. This is particularly relevant for the tougher situations (curses) in life.

Chapter 47

Establishing objective clarity

Situation to address

Delivering a strategy, presents a whole range of situations, especially for the CEO, who is ultimately sitting on the "top of the pyramid".

Responding wrongly, or inappropriately, can not only be ineffective but can also cause "ripple impact" damages.

How should one assess a situation before responding or reacting to it?

What is the best way to approach situations at work, be they, on the face of it positive, or the more challenging and tough ones?

Suggested mindset and approach

Objectivity is the name of the game.

Pause, assess and <u>see</u> a situation for what it is.

When faced with a seemingly good or tough situation, be mindful and bring as much objectivity as possible when assessing and dealing with it.

By way of example:

- Right from the outset, start off by considering and "seeing", as objectively as possible, the situation for what it is. Especially from a moral and "core values" perspective.
- Confirm whether your perspective is consistent with others.
- Develop collective and collaborative objective input to keep the facts on the table and encourage the dismissal of any misplaced or emotional assessment of the issue.

- Put any related decisions into context.
  - For a good/positive situation, was it because of luck or skill?
  - In a tough situation, consider if it is as "tough" as you think.
- Develop an "appreciation" mind-set. Are the "good news" aspects taken for granted?
- For seemingly tough situations develop a clear and positive mind-set, seeing the good within, including an "it will be good at the end of the day" approach. Avoid any negative "why me" questions and remind yourself that things could be worse
- Acknowledge the "lucky breaks" experienced - put the challenging situation in context

Results and benefits

Benefits from adopting an objective mind-set to situations include:

- Faster, relevant and more effective 'quality value' based approaches and decisions.
- Collaborative objectivity which enables the chosen way forward to be executed and put into place faster and more effectively.
- Greater appreciation and recognition of the positive aspects and how they can be utilized as part of the solution.
- Bringing perspective to challenges, avoiding wrong decisions through misplaced fear or concerns. Fear and panic are replaced by clear sighted objectivity and context, which can be focused on the issue at hand.
- When faced with a tough situation, by "thinking good", positive and constructive approaches tend to be adopted which, in turn, tend to deliver more positive outcomes.

Impact takeaway

When the going gets tough, the tough get objective!

Making it personal – consider:

1. How have "tough" situations been identified and dealt with in the past?

2. Are "good" or positive situations also recognized and appreciated, in order to put any "tough" situations in perspective?
3. Were any feelings of "fear or panic" replaced by an objective assessment of the situation and options?
4. How could an "objective" approach be more effectively adopted in similar situations going forward?

My role model "shout outs" who...

➢ "Objectively assess every situation."

Insight from Torah Portion 48 – "Shoftim"

Situation:
Guidance on settling the land of Israel is given, including an instruction not to unnecessarily destroy trees. The reason given is:

Quote from the Torah:
Deuteronomy 20:19 – "… For a person is a tree in the field…"

Chassidic Insight:
This is the first and only time where the Torah describes what a person is. But why compare a person to a tree?

A tree is unique in that, whilst alive, it never stops growing. This is apparent from the rings found in a cross-section of a tree trunk, where each ring represents a year of growth.

Whilst some rings indicate a year of significant growth, (when the rings are far apart) and others less (when the rings are closer to one another), each ring indicates at least some element of growth regardless of the tree's environment or its conditions.

In addition to this, every year all trees give off "countless" (hundreds or even thousands) of fruit or seeds.

From this we learn that every human being has the opportunity to <u>continuously</u> grow, develop and improve, regardless of circumstances.

Furthermore, the <u>potential</u> impact made by each individual is <u>always</u> huge, as represented by the "countless" fruit or seeds generated by a tree each year.

Every individual can always grow and contribute additional impact until their very last day… in fact, trees typically produce larger and larger "crops" as they age, which should inspire one to contribute more each year than the last.

Chapter 48

Demotivated? Feeling stuck? Nowhere to go?

Situation to address

Strategy and goals delivered? Or even at the top of your game with nowhere else to grow?

Or even on a personal level feeling demotivated or stuck in a rut?

What should you do when it feels like there's nowhere to progress to?

Suggested mindset and approach

Know that you always have the potential to grow and increase your impact. Understanding that, how do you deal with any limiting beliefs?

Of most importance is realizing that you have unlimited personal growth and development potential. There is always more room for improvement and to have greater impact across the multiple facets of your role and responsibilities.

Recognize that even small changes or actions can have significant impact and resonance (just like one small seed can create a whole tree which, itself, can create many more seeds).

Contemplate everything you do in your role, breaking it down across many heads, ranging from, for example, interpersonal ("greetings and meetings"), to execution.

Consider "out of the box" ideas where a real difference can be made.

Every role and function has room for improvement, from how decisions are made through to how they are implemented and optimized.

Expand your realm of knowledge to stimulate ideas. Identify the various sources of additional information, to learn from, and generate inspiration for further growth and improvement.

These can obviously include "structured" sources such as printed material and courses, to more informal ones like interacting with role models or even self-reflection.

Track and measure your performance (quarterly, annually) to reinforce and reaffirm to yourself how you can always grow.

Finally, and for some most importantly, identify areas <u>outside</u> of "work" where you can make a positive contribution. This is especially true for the more experienced individuals… who like "older trees" have even greater potential impact to offer – experience and wisdom for example.

Results and benefits

Even when strategic goals are delivered, more can always be done.

Within your career, regardless of whether you have the same job title, output and impact can be continuously developed and transformed.

Appreciating that every day offers an opportunity to grow, enables you to feel truly alive and full of purpose, leading to a greater impact.

In addition to this is the inevitable knock-on effect to others, be they inside or outside of work, inspiring them to make the most of life, helping them grow.

Having a continuous "growth mentality" can arguably be one of the most significant "untouched" levers to positively impacting both individuals, whether emotionally or financially.

One might even find that a dead-end job could facilitate the time and energy for meaningful personal growth outside of the work environment.

Impact takeaway

You can always <u>significantly</u> grow your impact and develop as an individual. So, what are you waiting for?

Making it personal – consider:

1. Ever felt "stuck" or stagnant in a role? If so, why? Is there any complacency or despondency?
2. What are the potential areas for improvement or greater impact be it in or out of the workplace?
3. How can I grow this year compared to last?
4. What specific actions can I take to "up my game" both in and out of the workplace?

My role model "shout outs" who…

➢ "Always demonstrates a growth mindset."

Insight from Torah Portion 49 – "Ki Teitzei"

Situation:
Advice on how to settle the land continues, including how to approach battles.

Quote from the Torah:
*Deuteronomy 21:10 – "When you go **out** to war **upon** your enemies,…"*

Chassidic Insight:
Why not just say "When you go to war"… why include the unnecessary words "out" and "upon". Furthermore, doesn't one go "against" one's enemies rather than "upon"?

The concept of going to war, from a Torah perspective, specifically includes addressing your <u>personal challenges</u> in life. So, when it comes to tackling personal challenges (call it your demons), what do you learn from including the word "out"? Even more curious why say "upon" rather than the more usual phraseology "against"?

The word "out", implies that battling with a personal challenge is not the norm. It requires a process of going "outside" the norm of life and applying more effort and energy than is usual every day.

Secondly, going "upon" (i.e. from above), rather than "against" one's enemies, leads to an approach from a higher place. Namely, connecting your soul to God whilst in battle, taking a morally higher ground and a broader perspective.

Avoiding "going against", or, down to your enemies' level, reduces the risk of unnecessary aggression which can often result in compromising your values. Rather, going "upon" facilitates pity, compassion and maintaining composure, whilst still seeking victory.

Ultimately, the result of "stepping out" to a higher, more concerted effort, as well as developing a higher moral perspective, enables your challenges to be achieved with a "victory" not a vengeance mind-set. This also helps to elevate and teach the enemy (or the enemy within, the demons), rather than just eradicate it.

Chapter 49

How to win

Situation to address

Delivering a strategy inevitably requires dealing with many day-to-day battles.

In fact, there are times when almost everyone might have a personal battle at work.

This could include challenges such as dealing with your competitors in a sales pitch to seeking a new job or a promotion.

What is the most effective way of winning personal battles?

Suggested mindset and approach

Firstly, recognize that such situations require a different approach from other more regular, or normal, aspects in life. They require more effort and necessitate a more focused and determined mindset than other situations.

Secondly, try to see the bigger picture by adopting a moral perspective that avoids going down to your "competitors" or adversaries' level.

Avoid "direct" comparisons or criticisms.

Rather, take a moral higher ground. Develop an awareness as to your relative gifts, strengths and advantages and focus on levering these, as well as making them known and understood.

Essentially, position yourself based on your merits, in order to "stand above, or apart from, the crowd", rather than be compared to them on a "head-to-head" basis.

Results and benefits

Your strengths will shine through and stand out, whilst at the same time you put your best foot forward.

Your energy will not be wasted on meaningless "mud-slinging" or low impact efforts, but rather it will be optimized and focused on where you can make a positive impression and stand out.

Practically speaking, by being mindful of your "higher strengths", your special characteristics will be more clearly understood when you are facing a challenging situation.

A critical, additional, benefit to this approach is that you will come across calmer and more confident with an objective, clear, mindset… Thereby avoiding the pitfall of "emotive" comparisons, where you may come across in a negative, even divisive light.

As a result of all of this, you would be presenting yourself in the best possible way, thus optimizing your chances of "victory", as well as even winning the respect of the competition – a double win.

Finally, even if you were not to win in a particular situation, regardless of your positive and constructive approach, there would be a greater chance of being favourably considered in future interactions, because of the respect that you will have engendered.

Impact takeaway

Determined, focused, insightful and objective perspectives are powerful tools to spur on victory in the face of challenge.

Making it personal – consider:

1. In past competitive situations, was I focused on direct comparison, or did I focus on what makes me special?
2. Am I able to articulate my unique strengths?
3. How compelling can I be about *me*?
4. Am I able to step up to the plate and put in the required additional energy to win, in a way which focuses on my positive aspects?
5. What approach could I adopt next time I face a challenge or battle at work?

Part V - Delivering the Strategy and Mission

My role model "shout outs" who…

➤ "Takes the moral higher ground in all challenges."

Torah Insight from Portion 50 – "Ki Tavo"

Situation:
Continuing the theme of settling the land of Israel, aspects of farming are now covered.

Quote from the Torah:
Deuteronomy 26:2,4 – *"you shall **take of the first of all the fruit** of the ground, which you will bring from your land, which the Lord, your God, is giving you. And you shall put [them] into a basket and go to the place which the Lord, your God, will choose to have His Name dwell there.... And the Kohen (priest) will take the basket from your hand, laying it before the altar of the Lord, your God."*

Chassidic Insight:
After all the sweat and toil of working the land in all sorts of conditions, from freezing cold to blistering heat, why is there the command to "give away" the first fruits, rather than enjoy them?

The answer is that showing gratitude and appreciation should be the first response to achieving success in your pursuits, whatever they may be.

Not just in words, but actual deeds. In fact, giving away the <u>very first fruits</u>, rather than enjoying them yourself, is the most authentic act of showing sincere appreciation.

At the heart of this, you need to acknowledge and be reminded that the resulting fruit crops are never solely through your own efforts.

Namely, we need to appreciate the help, gifts and miracles of nature that we are given.

This acknowledgment enables a sense of gratitude and humility, removing the egotistical view of "look what I did", and thereby making space for more blessings and success.

Chapter 50

Managing success ...what to do after you win

Situation to address

What should you do after delivering a success?

How should you feel and celebrate?

Most importantly, especially as CEO, how should you manage success so that once achieved it continues and grows?

Suggested mindset and approach

Show gratitude and appreciation. Not just in words, but action.

Central to this is the acknowledgement that despite your efforts, there were other factors at play, which led to the successful outcome. In fact, it would be delusional and damaging to think otherwise.

Standing back and identifying all the various factors and dependencies which played a part (critical or otherwise), and which led to the overall success.

Through this understanding and reflection, you are best placed to meaningfully acknowledge and thank the other people and factors that contributed to the successful outcome.

Expressing gratitude should not just be by words alone, but by some form of concrete action. Ideally sharing in some way, the "fruits of success".

Critically this should not be delayed too long but should be offered at the first opportunity, after the successful outcome is clear.

Finally, the concept of "appreciating success" need not be limited to only major goals as it is equally relevant to minor successes.

You should thus also identify and appreciate those involved in "small wins" too.

Results and benefits

Prompt acknowledgment and sharing of success binds together all those team members who were part of the journey.

Acknowledgement is a clear expression of humility. It also removes "damaging" self-absorbed ego from the success/win.

More importantly, this action orientated gratitude and "collaborative celebration" can generate higher motivation from everyone involved, inspiring them to continued drive for success, going forward.

The sooner the appreciation is acknowledged, the faster the higher commitment and motivation from team members occurs. Furthermore, sincere, early and tangible "first fruit" sharing indicates confidence and high aspiration for the success still to come.

Failing to acknowledge soon enough can result in people feeling unappreciated and taken for granted. This, in turn, could result in reduced motivation at a critical point, when the potential for continued success and growth is at its peak.

Adopting this approach for "small wins" as well as major ones will help form, nurture and create, a "win minded" culture, which itself can fuel endless future "fruits" for the organization.

Impact takeaway

Waste no time in acknowledging and sharing success in a concrete way to all those who played a role.

Making it personal – consider:

1. Think about recent successes. How did I demonstrate appreciation and acknowledgement to all those who were involved?
2. How was appreciation shown by my superiors when successes were achieved?
3. Were the "success gifts" and acknowledgments meaningful to the recipients?

4. Going forward how could appreciation be shown more promptly and meaningfully both by myself to others and others to me?
5. How can this be developed for small wins as well as major ones in order to build a win minded culture?

My role model "shout outs" who...

➢ "Immediately shares success with all those involved."

Torah Insight from Portion 51 – "Nitzavim"

Situation:
Moses shares that in the future the people of Israel will, at times, make wrong decisions and go astray.

Moses then explains that they will eventually learn how to make the right decisions.

Quote from the Torah:
*Deuteronomy 30:19 – ".. I have set before you life and death, the blessing and the curse. You shall **choose life**…"*

Chassidic Insight:
*Isn't it obvious that one would prefer to **choose** life over death? So why would Moses "waste his breath" by stating something so obvious?*

The power of free choice is not something that should be taken for granted. It is a uniquely human capability and needs to be continuously and carefully utilized.

There are also several deeper aspects and messages regarding what is meant by "life", in making choices and decisions, including:

- *Choosing life implies not just making the "right" decision but also choosing options which will enable you to live a more meaningful life, aligned to higher purposes and values.*
- *This implies not focusing on short-term, immediate gratification and material cravings, but rather opting for more sustainable "life value", positive impact options.*
- *Finally, once a decision is made you need to bring it to "life", to live it, with the appropriate commitment and energy to make it happen.*

CHAPTER 51

The art of making strategic decisions

Situation to address

Executing a strategy is full of choices and decisions – sometimes big ones!.

On what basis should they be made?... and once made how should they be embraced?

Suggested mindset and approach

The first step is to try and identify all potential options and potential choices.

Then, selecting the 'right' one should be driven by a conscious mindset of what is "truly right".

Namely, which "value based" options are most likely to result in delivering the most sustainable, positive impact to the organization.

Importantly, choosing the "most positive" options should be based on meaningful, long-term values, not just on quick win financial returns. It's not (always) about choosing the option with the quickest short-term profit.

Once the decision is made, it needs to be "activated"… namely, actioned with energy and determination in order to realize the desired outcome. After all, a decision is nothing without the appropriate follow through action and determined focus to achieve its objectives.

Results and benefits

First and foremost, a "value based" decision approach cultivates positive ethos which people usually want to be a part of.

This, in turn, also sharpens and reinforces clear and compelling mission statements, which themselves form and develop high impact strategies.

Critical to this is adopting a positive mind-set to all decisions. As already discussed, this, in turn, creates a positive environment, which itself breeds positive outcomes.

All these aspects further enhance creating a culture of meaningful actions and dynamism which, as well as driving success, tends to attract skilled, ambitious and motivated employees.

Ultimately, this "values based" approach will enhance the very "life" and sustainability of the organization and your team's desire to be part of it.

Impact takeaway

Making the right decisions based on appropriate values rather than just short-term financial gain, results in optimizing long-term financial returns and impact.

Making it personal – consider:

1. On what basis should decisions be made? Are they ever driven by short-term/quick win or self-interest factors?
2. How proud do I feel about such decisions? What was the long-term positive impact?
3. What are *my* true values? Are they the bedrock of all decisions and choices?
4. How can my next major choice/decision embrace these values?

My role model "shout outs" who…

➤ "Consistently makes value based decisions, rather than on short-term financial benefit."

Torah Insight from Portion 52 – "Vayelech"

Situation:
The last day of Moses's life has now arrived.

Quote from the Torah:
Deuteronomy 31:1,2 - "And Moses **went**, and he spoke the following words to all Israel. He said to them, "Today I am one hundred and twenty years old. I can no longer go or come,…""

Chassidic Insight:
The word "went" (Vayelech), seems superfluous. The Torah could just have written "And Moses spoke..". Furthermore, what has this got to do with his 120th birthday falling on the last day of his life?

The word Vayelech (went), connotes forward movement. Not just a marginal shift but, rather, a real and noticeable move forward.

From this we learn how Moses, even on his very last day, had energy and drive to take major strides and move forward in what he was chosen to do, namely, to lead the people. He made the effort to gather them all for one last message.

Thus, <u>until the very end,</u> he was focused on his mission and purpose in life, reaching new heights, moving forward and continuously progressing with stamina and ambition. In this way, he was a role model in how to maximise the gift of life and, despite already realizing amazing achievements, chose not to rest on his laurels. Rather, Moses made every day count, with an aim to progress further.

Passing away on one's birthday implies the completion of a life which was lived to the fullest. The day of one's birth is a time of excitement and joy regarding the potential that has been brought to life. The time of one's passing is the assessment, acknowledgement and "celebration" of what potential was ultimately realized. The more one is focused on continuously moving forward in life, the more there will be to celebrate.

In this respect we learn that Moses optimized his life's impact right up until his very last day.

Chapter 52

How to "max out" on your potential impact

Situation to address

After having a successful track record of achievements, what next?

Even if successful, are you on "auto pilot"?

How can you keep on going to **fully** realize your potential in life, rather than falling short of what could have been realized?

Suggested mindset and approach

Appreciating the potential value and impact of each day is critical.

Avoid going into "auto pilot" when approaching a new day. Rather, start every day with a fresh perspective by pausing and reflecting.

If you feel that you've reached the end of the road using your skills and attributes in one avenue, consider how you can apply them in another, "today".

Recognize the gift of another day. Acknowledge how every moment is unique and offers opportunity for your individual growth and impact.

Contemplate what you would like to achieve today... not just in output but also behaviours. What are your ambitions for the day... how would you like to impact, shift and improve your realm of influence by the end of the day compared to the start?

Consciously and purposefully prioritize actions of those which are most urgent and impactful. Balance those which have immediate results as well as those delivering long term goals.

Consider, were you to be graded on the day's performance, what would it take to achieve a top grade?

Now go out and do it... then, repeat, every day!

Results and benefits

This approach avoids the risk of resting on your laurels and thus missing potential opportunities to make significant additional positive contributions.

In short it enables you to "max out" on your abilities and unique gifts rather than take them for granted.

The impact that you can realize by having this approach can inspire others, resulting in a multiplier effect on positive outcomes. It becomes a virtuous circle.

Critically, this mindset can also motivate you to "pivot" your life into new fields, even if you have already reached a peak in this, your current, field. Furthermore, it avoids people feeling like "has-beens" and worthless, which can otherwise often be the signal given from high achievers to others.

In addition to this, yesterday's ambitions and goals grow to become different and more aspiring ones, rather than slowing down or halting. This brings closer into focus the realization of the "endless" potential that lies within.

Finally, the ongoing positive impact and influence, even after ones passing, is certainly enhanced and perpetuated by taking this approach, as touched on in chapter 5 "How to make a lasting impact".

(By way of example, and most notably, the Lubavitcher Rebbe, was renowned for his unceasing energy and determination. Not only did he achieve more from the age of 50 until his passing at 92, but since his passing the number of Chabad centres - and their global impact - more than doubled!)

Impact takeaway

Never stop being the best "you"... Every new day offers opportunities for transformational impact. Don't waste it!

Making it personal – consider:

1. How do I approach each day? Ever feel like it's "just another day"?
2. How could this mindset be pivoted to enable a "fresh" and ambitious approach?
3. Where, and how, have you achieved your ambitions?
4. How can these be built upon and progressed to the next level? … and what should they be?
5. What does tomorrow look like now?

My role model "shout outs" who…

➢ "Give their best at all time."

Torah Insight from Portion 53 – "Haazinu"

Situation:

The intensity and critical importance of Moses' words were ever increasing as the moment of his passing draws closer. So much so, that he composes a poem to communicate major, critical messages that needed to be actioned after his passing. The first line of this poem is:

Quote from the Torah:

Deuteronomy 32:1 – "**Listen** (Haazinu), O heavens, and I will speak! And let the earth **hear** the words of my mouth!"

Chassidic Insight:

There are a couple of aspects that arise from this curious opening line of Moses' intense final message, namely:

1. What's the difference between "listening" and "hearing" (why not just use one term or the other)?

2. Why refer to <u>both</u> heaven and earth? ... why not just concentrate on either heaven or earth... and why does heaven come first?

The term "listen", in Hebrew, Haazinu, implies a close proximity to the entity with which you are communicating. (Haazinu literally means "give ear"... namely a form of whispering in the ear).

Whereas "hear", implies a long distance between the two parties, such as "can you hear me from where you are?"

This phrase that Moses uses implies that he had a closer proximity to Heaven than Earth, as the term "listen" was used for Heaven.

From this we learn that when it comes to critically important messages, ambitions or goals, (which was what the poem contained), you need to <u>start developing them from a "big picture" heavenly perspective.</u>

However, these aspects should not be so idealistic, making them impractical, and out of touch with reality. Rather, the messages still need to be "heard" and implemented in practice on earth, and so have a real purpose to them, otherwise they would be pointless.

Chapter 53
Setting the mission and ambitions

Situation to address

Articulated mission statements, goals, values and strategic ambitions normally set the "ultimate" ideal, result and desired outcome.

How can one ensure they can be appropriately ambitious, yet tangible and practically implementable, in order to deliver the greatest potential impact and benefit?

Suggested mindset and approach

Heaven mindset:

First off, "listen closely" and understand what is going on in the outside world. Objectively acknowledge the broader picture.

From this perspective, think BIG regarding vision, impact, purpose and goals, be it for yourself or your organization, from a reaching for the stars / heavenly perspective.

Put yourself in an "out of the box" mindset. Share your thoughts and surround yourself with visionaries and strategic thinkers.

In doing this, define your vision, purpose and goals so that they will have a sustainable and timeless relevance. Consider many of the benefits rather than just a few (financial) ones.

Establish core values and principles which match these ambitions.

<u>Earth mindset:</u>
Then ask yourself "so what".... Namely, how can this be realized and what are the first key steps which will most likely deliver the vision.

"Hear" what the practical "earthly" aspects of implementation look like.

One thus shifts from big picture "potential" to the nitty gritty of implementation.

Of course, one needs to be mindful of where one is right now... and how this can be sensibly developed towards the vision.

Identify what should be actioned and set out the steps, both short and medium term, that need to be taken to achieve the vision.

Finally, and importantly, repeat the "listening/hearing" process at appropriate intervals and realign when either there have been significant external changes, or medium term goals have been implemented.

Results and benefits

Adopting this "strategic" approach, directs you towards, and eventually realize, long term sustainability, and paths of maximum impact, achieving your potential and purpose.

Avoid aiming too low, and thus underperforming, as well as setting unrealistically, over stretched goals, which cannot be implemented.

By constantly being mindful of the optimal vision and end goals, you avoid being complacent, or stuck on a path where the benefits become eroded over time.

As a result, you can realize the best of both worlds, steering towards reaching for the stars whilst not getting lost in ethereal concepts but, rather, translating visions into practical, grounded and realistic actions, which will lead to success.

Essentially, if approached properly, by adopting a broad set of values and "impact" aspirations, you will ultimately deliver far greater sustainable value, including financial results.

Continuous alignment of goals, relevant to what is happening in an ever changing outside world, is critical to ultimate success – adapt or die!

This not only reduces the risk of becoming redundant but, rather, enables survival even in the face of the most challenging changes, to deliver sustainable and growing impact.

Impact takeaway

Heaven to earth is the pathway to "**forever** thrive and survive".

Making it personal – consider:

1. What are my long term goals, visions and ambitions?
2. What are they founded and based upon? Just financial parameters, or a broader set of "big thinking" impacts?
3. Do they really reflect my ultimate potential? Will their relevance last the test of time?
4. What steps can I take to recalibrate the true potential of what I do?
5. How would a "heaven to earth" process look like for me? … and when will I start?

My role model "shout outs" who…

➢ "Think "big", yet keep it practical and actionable."

Torah Insight from Portion 54 – "Vezot Habracha"

Situation:

In this last portion of the Torah, Moses passes away. The Torah concludes by praising him, stating that there was "no other prophet who arose in Israel like Moses". The <u>final</u> words of the Torah are:

Quote from the Torah:

Deuteronomy 34:10-12 – "…which Moses performed before the eyes of all Israel."

Chassidic Insight:

Out of all the incredulous events of his life, what exactly did Moses "perform before the eyes of all the people"?

The sages explain that it was "before the eyes of all of Israel", that Moses broke the first tablets of stone on which the Ten Commandments were engraved.

He broke them after a small fringe group committed the sin of idol worship, by praying to a statue of a golden calf. (In addition to this the people as a whole sinned, by doing nothing to stop them.

Because God told Moses (Exodus 32:10) "I will annihilate them, and I will make you into a great nation…", Moses smashed the tablets into fragments, in order to prevent any incrimination on the people.

He did this to "tear up and annul the contract" between God and the people, so as to cancel any obligation against idol worship, and thus remove any threat of punishment or destruction of the people.

So why end the Torah with a reminder of this disappointing event? Why was this considered to be Moses' most praiseworthy act which merited the final chapter?

What lessons are so important here, that they are worthy of ending the Torah with this event?

In many ways up until that point, Moses going to receive the tablets of stone which "God had written", represented the peak of his life's achievements… And yet Moses destroyed them before the whole people, even just for the sake of a few individuals who had practiced idol worship.

*He did this because he understood that **his purpose was more important than his achievements**. His purpose was that of leader of all the people, to develop and build the people for their future, to do whatever it took to protect them.*

*Thus, in his **humility** and sense of purpose, Moses smashed the tablets to "tear" and annul the contract with God, to protect the people from any retribution and punishment from their sin, even if this was effectively "destroying" his greatest personal achievement.*

It is this lesson which he gave <u>before the eyes</u> of all the people, namely, to always put your purpose and value before your own personal achievements.

This therefore became the final lesson for all the people, in order to ultimately survive as a people, each individual must have both the strength and the humility to focus their life on their unique purpose and mission, rather than dwell on their achievements.

This is the lesson which is most relevant today in order to have a meaningful life and an elevating impact upon the world. The knowledge that we are physically just made of dust, but by harnessing our soul's mission and purpose, rather than dwelling on personal achievements, we can have an everlasting impact.

Finally, by way of note, following the atonement of all of Israel for the sin of idol worship a second, even more valuable, set of tablets was given to Moses. Thus, putting aside your personal achievements enables even more to be realized and accomplished.

Chapter 54

Personal achievement versus team purpose

Situation to address

What's more important, your personal achievements or realizing your true purpose for the "greater good"?

Often these are aligned, however, what should you do if they are conflicted, especially for the CEO/leader of an organization?

Moreover, in order to deliver the overall strategic goals, what if personal achievements need to be "thrown away" in order to achieve your purpose for the "greater good"?

Suggested mindset and approach

Whilst easier said than done, despite the lure of your personal achievements your personal purpose, mission and ultimate responsibility to others should never be compromised, even if it requires "throwing away" your greatest achievements.

In many ways this requires a mind-set of unrelenting humility and clarity, recognizing that choosing a path to fulfil your purpose is at the heart of what should govern your choices and actions.

Understanding the difference between, "look what I have achieved", to "this is my ultimate purpose" is critical and resonates to the message in chapter 1, namely, to focus on elevating the corner of the world where you are, to a better place, rather than "just" accumulating wealth and personal achievements.

Of course, the clearer you understand your purpose and core values, the easier it will be to focus on your purpose rather than on your personal achievements.

Results and benefits

With this humble, selfless, approach you will ultimately be able to realize far more of your purpose, rather than be held back by holding onto, or dwelling, on personal achievements.

In fact, by "sacrificing" achievements for the sake of purpose, you are setting yourself up for even greater impact and personal achievements.

At a bare minimum this mind-set avoids the risk of being satisfied with your achievements, and thus not being further inspired to continue pursuing your potential impact and purpose.

Such selfless action will not go unnoticed and, without question, will profoundly impact and inspire all those around you, to understand the importance of meaningful purpose versus personal achievement.

This alone will help embed priceless behaviours and cultural values on both an individual and organizational perspective.

Ultimately, as and when personal achievements need to be displaced, for the sake of purpose, it creates the greatest opportunity to embed your true mission and deliver significant and long-lasting meaningful impact.

In many ways it is an opportunity to take you and those around you to the next level.

In conclusion, as we started to discuss in Chapter 1, by making this choice you will have elevated the dust that you are made of to the greatest heights, and further advance the ultimate purpose of your work-life and career. And, just like the Torah, the minute we finish we start it all over again……

Impact takeaway

Putting your purpose over personal achievements, elevates your "dust" to the greatest heights.

Making it personal – consider:

1. How committed am I to my true purpose?
2. Which achievements am I most proud of?
3. Would I dismantle these achievements to further advance my ultimate and meaningful purpose?
4. Are there any achievements that stand in the way of what I could do to make an even greater impact?
5. How could I push these achievements aside to deliver greater impact and "take things to the next level"?

My role model "shout outs" who...

➢ "Exhibits humility and commitment in doing what needs to be done for the benefit of all."